The Stranger as My Guest

The Stranger as My Guest

A Critical Anthropology of Hospitality

Michel Agier

Translated by Helen Morrison

polity

Originally published in French as *L'étranger qui vient. Repenser l'hospitalité* © Éditions du Seuil, 2018

This English edition © 2021 by Polity Press

Polity Press
65 Bridge Street
Cambridge CB2 1UR, UK

Polity Press
101 Station Landing
Suite 300
Medford, MA 02155, USA

ISBN-13: 978-1-5095-3988-8- hardback
ISBN-13: 978-1-5095-3989-5- paperback

A catalogue record for this book is available from the British Library.

Library of Congress Cataloging-in-Publication Data
Names: Agier, Michel, 1953- author. | Morrison, Helen (Langauge
translator), translator.
Title: The stranger as my guest : a critical anthropology of hospitality /
Michel Agier ; translated by Helen Morrison.
Other titles: Étranger qui vient. English
Description: Cambridge, UK ; Medford, MA, USA : Polity Press, 2021. |
"Originally published in French as L'étranger qui vient. Repenser
l'hospitalité, Edition du Seuil, 2018 ." | Includes bibliographical
references and index. | Summary: "A well-argued case for a new
hospitality policy that welcomes foreigners as guests rather than
treating them as aliens or enemies"-- Provided by publisher.
Identifiers: LCCN 2020028924 (print) | LCCN 2020028925 (ebook) | ISBN
9781509539888 (hardback) | ISBN 9781509539895 (paperback) | ISBN
9781509539901 (epub) | ISBN 9781509544929 (adobe pdf)
Subjects: LCSH: Hospitality. | Immigrants--Government policy. |
Refugees--Government policy. | Emigration and immigration--Social
aspects. | Strangers.
Classification: LCC GT3410 .A4313 2021 (print) | LCC GT3410 (ebook) | DDC
395.3--dc23
LC record available at https://lccn.loc.gov/2020028924
LC ebook record available at https://lccn.loc.gov/2020028925

Typeset in 11 on 13pt Sabon
by Fakenham Prepress Solutions, Fakenham, Norfolk NR21 8NL
Printed and bound in Great Britain by CPI Group (UK) Ltd, Croydon

For further information on Polity, visit our website:
politybooks.com

Contents

Acknowledgements

This essay is the result of various encounters. I would like to thank Patrick Boucheron and Alain Prochiantz for inviting me to take part in the symposium 'Migrations, asile, exil' ('Migration, Asylum, Exile') held at the Collège de France in November 2016, where my ideas on the social form and the politics of hospitality began to take shape. Cyrille Hanappe and the whole team at Actes & Cité invited me to participate in their project on 'La Ville accueillante' ('The Welcoming City') organised by PUCA (Plan Urbanisme Construction Architecture) and by Ville de Grand-Synthe, thereby allowing me to discover the practical issues around municipal hospitality. My thanks to the whole team. Alain Policar offered me the opportunity to explore cosmopolitanism, in the company of a range of philosophers, for an issue (201) of the journal *Raison Présente* for 2017 and for a symposium on the same subject, 'Cosmopolitisme ou barbarie?' ('Cosmopolitanism or Barbarity?') (Cevipof/ Sciences Po, June 2018): I am deeply grateful to him. Reflections on the theme of becoming a stranger and cinematographic representations of the subject were presented at the Festival des 3 Continents/Cinémas d'Afrique, d'Amérique Latine et d'Asie (Nantes, October 2017). My thanks go in particular to Claire Allouche, the programme planner, and to Jêrôme Baron, the artistic director, for their invitation.

This essay is based on discussions held in the context of the Babels research programme (Agence nationale de la recherche, 2016–19): our focus was on what has been referred to as 'the migration crisis', and we drew on research conducted in the field, largely open workshops, and short essays published by Éditions du passage clandestine in the series 'Bibliothèque des frontières', which I codirect with Stefan Le Courant. I would like to thank the forty or so researchers, students, and representatives from the voluntary sector who together made up the Babels collective from which I drew the inspiration and the enthusiasm for this book. Finally, it was in the context of my course 'Anthropologies de l'hospitalité' ('Anthropologies of Hospitality'), held at the École des hautes études en sciences sociales during the years 2016/17 and 2017/18, that the overall concept for this book gradually emerged. I thank the many people who participated in such a lively manner, and to my colleagues who brought us their own insight.

Finally, I would like to thank Bruno Auerbach at Éditions du Seuil for his attentive and perceptive reading of the French manuscript.

Introduction

Hospitality When Least Expected

Since the stranger who is my guest, the one arriving now, is by definition an outsider, someone who has literally come from outside, there is always the risk that, in that first glimpse, no matter how distant or indistinct that person's silhouette appears, he or she will be seen as an intruder by the people who witness that arrival, even though this would not be the stranger's own perception. Hospitality represents a response to this ambiguity, to the doubts and uncertainties that stem from it. It is the moment where a single gesture can transform the stranger into a guest, even if he or she still continues to be a stranger to some extent, and therefore continues to embody certain elements of the intruder. It is through the various manifestations and experiences of this practice of hospitality (still to be defined in the details of its implementation, its impact and its limitations) that each individual gradually forms their own conception of the stranger, of the different rules and regimes and of the extent of their strangeness, and therefore of the relationship that can be forged with him or her, both during and beyond the initial gesture of hospitality. Whatever its limitations in time and space, this 'space–time' of hospitality is a vital element in determining the nature of the ensuing relationship.

The observations made by the philosopher Jean-Luc Nancy on the intruder as a foreign body that is 'grafted' onto and into my own body provide the most concrete and comprehensive starting point from which to approach the problem, along with some ideas for its eventual solution:

> Something of the stranger has to intrude, or else he loses his strangeness. If he already has the right to enter and stay, if he is awaited and received, no part of him being unexpected or unwelcome, then he is not an intruder any more, but then neither is he any longer a stranger. To exclude all intrusiveness from the stranger's coming is therefore neither logically acceptable nor ethically admissible.
>
> If, once he is there, he remains a stranger, then for as long as this remains so [...] his coming does not stop: he continues to come and his coming does not stop intruding in some way [...] a disturbance, a trouble in the midst of intimacy.
>
> We have to think this through, and therefore to put it into practice: the strangeness of the stranger would otherwise be reabsorbed – would be an issue no longer – before he even crossed the threshold. To welcome a stranger, moreover, is necessarily to experience his intrusion. For the most part, we would rather not admit this [...] This moral correctness presupposes that, upon receiving the stranger, we efface his strangeness at the threshold: it aims thereby not to have received him at all. But the stranger insists and intrudes. This fact is hard to receive and perhaps to conceive.[1]

The sense of intrusion that Nancy is trying to capture here emerges in the context of a highly complex heart transplant operation, followed by a raft of complications over a period of many years. The philosopher has drawn on this experience to produce a powerful work on identity and the stranger, on what is ours and what is different, on the inside and the outside that will be useful here (although any substantial analogies should be avoided). Let us see how this works.

The two concepts of guest and of stranger must not be confused if we wish to be able to describe, according to the anthropological tradition, what is meant by *making the stranger a guest* ('[i]f he already has the right to enter and stay, if he is awaited and received, no part of him being unexpected or unwelcome', then 'he is not an intruder any more'). This also means that, for us, hospitality represents a test ('[t]o welcome a stranger, moreover, is necessarily to experience his intrusion'). It is not a matter of behaving as though the stranger were not a stranger, so that 'we efface his strangeness at the threshold'. It is, on the contrary, a matter of acknowledging, on the basis of the sense of intrusion experienced, the very *political* dimension of hospitality, which involved making the decision to offer the stranger a welcome. It is a solution to a potential conflict (hostility towards intrusion), but a temporary solution, which has a beginning and an end. For, '[i]f, once he is there, he remains a stranger, then for as long as this remains so [...] his coming does not stop', nor will it stop being 'a disturbance, a trouble in the midst of intimacy'. We need therefore to step outside the space and time accorded to hospitality. Later, after many years – as Nancy tells us, speaking of the foreign body that was transplanted into his own and enabled him to live longer – the intruder ceases to be an intruder, but I myself have changed, I am both the same and another.

It is this combination of paradoxes, of tensions and ambiguities that is revealed by the gestures and the efforts made all over Europe, in the name of hospitality, in the face of what has been called 'the migrant crisis', which I identify as being, more fundamentally, a crisis of the nation states in response to the challenges posed by increased mobility.

From the year 2000 onwards, and especially since 2015, the majority of European countries have seen a divergence between national governments and some of their citizens on the subject of the welcome extended to migrants and refugees. On the one hand, governments have sought to demonstrate a certain protectiveness towards their citizens by portraying migrants as a threat to the security and identity of their countries, reviving a symbolic theme highlighted a few years ago by the American philosopher Wendy Brown[2] – namely that of the strong (and masculine) state protecting the fragile (feminine) nation... Walls, expulsions, mass checks, a dissuasive police presence, all intended to reassure nervous inhabitants, and they were ready to give up some of their own freedom when confronted with the spectre of the dangerous stranger, who would thus be kept at a distance. In France in particular, the lack of enthusiasm or expertise demonstrated by government authorities in providing a dignified and peaceful welcome to migrants and refugees and the confusion provoked by the arrival of migrants to Paris, Ventimiglia or Calais – admittedly on a large, though by no means overwhelming or catastrophic scale – seem to have been both a response to, and a way of nurturing, a widely felt anxiety of the sort most clearly expressed by parties of the extreme right. In accordance with the supposed expectation of the population at large, there was a clear need to demonstrate all possible reticence and distrust towards the intruder, which meant not providing shelters, reassurance or food, all of which could have been made available, from a material and economic standpoint, without any special difficulty. And yet this same attitude provoked another section of the population to act in precisely the opposite manner. Some people felt deeply concerned by the state of the world and by the hostility displayed by their governments towards certain strangers (comments made by certain elites and images of neglect or of police violence). These people wanted to take action rather than remain indifferent, to show solidarity to the peoples or individuals in danger, the ones they were seeing arriving in their immediate neighbourhood, coming across their mountains, onto their coasts, into their streets. As a result, it has become possible – and by no means uncommon – to join forces and criticise states from a standpoint of hospitality, at a societal, community-based or micro-local level. This politicization of hospitality is, as we shall see, an alternative way of defining the 'politics' of hospitality and of understanding the contemporary meaning of a practice at once ancient and constantly transforming.

The entire history of hospitality demonstrates that, through a gradual process, the responsibility – on a family, community, or local level – for the duties of hospitality has been distanced from society and instead delegated, and at the same time diluted, within the functions of the state. That responsibility has been replaced by the rights of asylum seekers or refugees. Subsequently these rights have themselves ended up being diluted in the politics of control over borders, territories and movement and are now so far removed from any general principle of hospitality that they have become virtually unrecognisable. This is what lies behind the 'resurgence' of hospitality that, in what might be described as a complete reversal of direction, goes from politics to society and from the latter to the private, domestic world.

So how do we go about rethinking hospitality in this new context? In order to grasp both what has been lost and what is now emerging, to understand the meaning of actions carried out in the name of hospitality associated with solidarity and politics, it is important to understand hospitality, in its current form, against the background of how it has long been portrayed by history and anthropology. We need to begin with a critical examination of the notion of 'unconditional hospitality' advocated notably by Jacques Derrida in the mid-1990s. Not that I fail to acknowledge the scale and the power of what, in the context of public debates, this strong injunction ('unconditional welcome') represents, but the conditions in which this 'unconditional' law is formulated and the impact it has, both on the host societies and on those to whom welcome is extended, need clarification.

Even though hospitality implies provisionally giving up some share of what by rights belongs to the host for the benefit of the guest (space, time, money, goods), we will need to identify the limits, both social and political, of this voluntary and unbalanced relationship, particularly when it is offered on an individual or local scale. What are these limits? Is it possible, desirable, and enough to *make the stranger my guest* in a world that is theoretically open and globalised but that, where human rights are concerned, remains closely tied to the national context? What impact can such a principle have in the light of the crisis faced by states confronted with contemporary migrations? A shift of focus from the standpoint of a local resident, citizen of a given national territory, who is offering welcome towards that of the individual who arrives, remains for a time, then stays or moves on – will lead us into a philosophical domain that is already rich, albeit still poor from a political point of view: that of cosmopolitan life.

Finally, a consideration of hospitality within a global context will logically take us to the central role occupied today by the 'stranger' – the one who becomes the guest within the relationship established by hospitality, the one who disappears as that absolute other, nameless, unreal and dehumanised (an *alien*) in the geopolitics of contemporary crises, or the one who arrives at my door today or tomorrow and who embodies the most ordinary, widespread and universal condition of the contemporary world. We will need therefore to rethink together the three principles of mobility (the outsider), of otherness (the stranger) and of belonging (the foreigner) in order to reflect on the stranger who is in all of us, to a greater or lesser degree; and, by doing so, we will place ourselves in a better position to understand our proximity to the radical, absolute and dehumanised stranger (alien) who is embodied in the other, but who, in a different historical context, could just as easily be myself.

The stranger who arrives at my door is the one who is there now, in my street, outside my house, the one I cannot leave to die of hunger or of cold without intervening in some way.

The stranger who arrives at my door is also a reference to this condition, increasingly widespread throughout the world, which means that we live in more than one society, in more than one culture, and which requires us to think differently about societies, cultures and each person's place within the world.

A final word before embarking on this journey, whose purpose is to explore and link theories and fields, philosophy and anthropology. Hospitality is an agreeable subject, and one on which a consensus is generally reached. For me, there are two reasons for this. The first is that we feel better about ourselves when we are able to see ourselves as welcoming and generous. The second is that hospitality calls on concepts of integration and focuses on an exchange of gift and counter-gift, of relationships and shared experiences. It is therefore a concept worth thinking about, yet one that it is difficult to put into practice. It is 'elusive', wrote René Schérer in 1993, in a text as erudite as it is flamboyant and indispensable to any consideration of hospitality; it 'slips from our grasp as soon as we try to restrict it to a single form, to capture it in an unequivocal sense. It is private and public, present and absent, welcoming and hypocritical; it takes many different forms and often appears precisely where it is least expected'.[3] For a more accurate portrayal, it should therefore be described in more concrete terms, whereupon it would inevitably transpire to be less beautiful, less kind, less consensual perhaps. But a discussion of the practice and politics that go under the name of hospitality might well lead us to implement concepts and conceptions of a better life for everyone, a peaceful life, and a life that is more egalitarian on the world scale. That would already take hospitality to another level.

1

Making the Stranger My Guest

If, in recent years, the notion of hospitality has reappeared in social debate in the context of the social sciences, and in particular of anthropology, it is because it is perceived to be in short supply. An ancient concept makes a comeback, but in an implicit form, as a question or as a protest triggered by the panic of European governments faced with the sudden surge in migrant numbers in 2015, then with the agreements between Europe and Turkey in March 2016 or between Italy and Libya in February 2017. These agreements were drawn up in order to keep out migrants, and even potentially those with legal status as 'refugees', as in the case of the Syrians or Eritreans who were turned away from European borders before any asylum applications could be made. The word of the law must be applied, and the law, insofar as it has stamped its name on what had previously been the subject of political debates and decisions, reminds us that its decrees could always take a different direction. For it is as a direct result of the law and of what it fails to address that citizens all across Europe, out of a sense of obligation and a conviction that they were in the right, have found themselves thinking and acting in ways that are often at odds with or in the place of the state.

As a result, examples of hospitality have re-emerged here and there, in a spontaneous, if slightly haphazard and ill-defined form. Some people have taken it upon themselves to welcome migrants into their homes without paying any attention to their legal status, thus transforming their gesture into an act of civil disobedience or, in the case of France, into a 'crime of solidarity' with attendant legal consequences.[1] The threat of sanctions destabilizes the apparent consensus surrounding hospitality, which is generally extolled as a virtue. Between morality and politics, between the implementation in a domestic context of personal convictions regardless of their broader significance and the championing of a welcoming and open society, the notion of hospitality conjures up all sorts of more or less coherent interpretations and a raft of different issues. As long as hospitality remains no more than a word and an abstraction, all is well. In reality, anthropologists and sociologists see more dissensus than consensus on the subject within their specific fields.

A first form of dissensus will involve us in a re-examination of the notion of unconditional hospitality. Of course, the words 'condition' and 'unconditional' have two possible meanings. In the first interpretation, I welcome you without condition, in other words without knowing who you are or where you come from, simply because your situation demands such an approach: this is the sense of the recurrent controversy that exists in France on the subject of unconditional access to medical treatment or to accommodation for the most vulnerable. 'Unconditional', this humanitarian or compassionate cause logically requires the other to be vulnerable before aid can be offered. In the second interpretation, I welcome you regardless of any conditions, that is, regardless of the contexts, places, systems, laws, and so on in which that welcome takes place: this is the sense of an ethical injunction, one that is decontextualized, deliberately freed from any dependence on place, one that exists by itself and is therefore sacred – a position defended in particular by the French philosopher Jacques Derrida.

We need in the first instance to examine and, if possible, to resolve this moral and political issue of unconditionality before we can attempt to understand in any detail the anthropological relationship that links the two sides, the one extending welcome and the one welcomed and that, in fact, turns out to be ... anything but unconditional. We will need therefore to look in detail at the conditions in which hospitality takes place and at its practical manifestations, whether it be in a domestic context (in my home), in the context of the close community (in my social group), or in that of the wider community (in my village, in my town).

The conditions of unconditionality

The claim that hospitality should be 'without conditions', that it should be imposed on everybody as a 'superior law' implies a definition of the stranger as an absolute entity, self-contained – in other words, sacred. In the 1990s, in order to oppose the stance taken by the current European policies on migration, Derrida drew inspiration from the traditions of ancient Greece, which allowed him to set out and to reiterate the duty of hospitality, taken in an absolute, pure, or infinite sense, with regard to the other, conceived of as equally absolute, unknown, anonymous – to use some of the adjectives chosen by the philosopher.[2] Many today vie with each other to invoke this 'duty of hospitality' as a fundamental truth without its being clear to whom exactly this exhortation is addressed. Is it meant for 'us', the citizens of Europe? Our governments? Our public institutions? All those countries where migrants arrive? Nor is there any consensus over the forms it is supposed to take – private or domestic, public, 'political'? And, in order to be really sure that this 'duty' is indeed self-evident, would it not make sense for such a 'superior law' to be set out in law? All these are matters worthy of clarification.

'Derrida made a translation error.' This is, in essence, the conclusion reached by Florence Dupont, an anthropologist of antiquity, in the context of an exercise that shifts the historical focus and enables a critical eye to be cast on the way certain contemporary concepts have emerged out of ancient Greek or Latin terms.[3] She is referring to the mistranslation of the word *xenos*, which according to her refers to the guest, one of the partners in a relationship of *xenia*, hospitality, and not, or at least not initially, the 'stranger', as we might be tempted to translate it in the light of our contemporary ideas and perceptions. If *xenos* is confused with the notion of the stranger as an entity, then hospitality should logically be separated from its practical manifestations and uses, and should be what might be described as 'unconditional' in order to take on a meaning associated with another fundamental definition, that of the foreigner stripped of any context. This is what Derrida did when the desire to defend a current cause led him to construct a transcendental definition of hospitality. Indeed, the philosopher ended up defending an argument that any anthropologist would consider excessively radical and disconcerting: 'These words "pure" and "infinite" [describing hospitality]', he acknowledges, 'convey unconditionality [...] Infinite, which goes with pure, simply indicates the fact that the other, who is not infinite, is nevertheless infinitely other. The other is implacably other, otherness cannot be measured: the other is utterly other.'[4] And such hospitality, a moral injunction stripped of any context, would clearly be extremely difficult to implement. Dupont, quite rightly, takes issue with 'essentialist philosophies' and their ontological abstractions formed 'from ancient words stripped of their practical meaning.[5] And yet, she goes on to say, the whole Greek concept of *xenia* is the very opposite of the 'gentle and kind' image attributed to it in the context of promoting the broader welcome of immigrants today.[6]

Is it possible to consider hospitality, both theoretically and in practical terms, without the one contradicting the other? Before proceeding with the anthropological investigation that this task involves, I should like to look a little more closely at some of the concepts involved, in order to restore the notion of unconditionality to its rightful place, in other words in the real world. Put another way, we are dealing here with the conditions of unconditionality.

In contrast with Derrida, Dupont focuses on the guest, *xenos*, or more precisely on the *condition* of being a guest, which is evidently very different from the identity of the stranger. For her, the guest (*xenos*) is defined in terms of a relationship: hospitality (*xenia*). The relationship comes first, and the *xenos* is not established per se outside this social relationship. 'It is not a case of the stranger being on the one side', she says, 'the host on the other, and this potential relationship of hospitality lying somewhere between the two. The stranger does not exist simply as a stranger: the person we call a stranger is either a guest or an enemy. The institution of hospitality defines a host and his or her guest, war defines an enemy and his or her enemy.'[7] He or she may indeed be a stranger in the sense of not speaking the same language as the host, and may well come from elsewhere; but what matters is that the conditions are set in place that enable a person to be treated as a guest, that is, as a relative or as a close friend. So, Dupont continues, in ancient Greek *xenos* has more to do with proximity, in other words with identity. In the same way, in anthropology the relationship might be seen as a form of acquaintanceship that reduces the sense of otherness, bringing together what was far apart. The linguist Émile Benveniste refers to this same relationship, *xenia*, as a 'pact',[8] namely the pact of hospitality: *xenos* is the partner in a pact of hospitality, and is therefore considered to be close to the host – already close, if I am welcoming a relation into my home, or rendered close through this pact, if he or she is someone unknown to me. Later, much later, in another context and in another era, the guest, *xenos*, will come to be referred to as a 'stranger', in the sense that he or she will be separated from the social foundations under which they were first recognized. It is in this way, Benveniste continues, that '*xenos*, so well characterized as "guest" in Homer, later became simply the "stranger", the non-national'.[9]

Derrida, too, had read Benveniste's well-known work *Indo-European Language and Society* and had noted the ambivalence of the word described by the linguist. But, he insisted, there would be not only ambivalence but also ambiguity, and even tension – on the one hand between the two conceptions of hospitality, unconditional or conditional, and on the other between the absolute nature of the stranger or the relational one associated with the condition of guest. It is true that today, at the beginning of the twenty-first century, these two meanings, unconditional–absolute and conditional–relational, are perceived as being contemporaneous and in competition with each other. What is to be done about this?

Without being in any way indifferent to moral values and to discussions around behaviours, the anthropologist is primarily interested in the fact that a relationship exists, and he or she therefore finds food for thought in this particular definition, that of the relationship of hospitality, rather than that of the absolute stranger per se. I am also interested to discover that *xenos*, which has come to designate the stranger, bears a trace of *xenia*, which still lingers. In *Of Hospitality*, Anne Dufourmantelle invites Derrida to elaborate on these words, which refer to hospitality and to the stranger, and he provides the following explanation:

> When Benveniste wants to define the *xenos*, there is nothing fortuitous in his beginning from the *xenia*. He inscribes the *xenos* in the *xenia*, which is to say in the pact, in the contract or collective alliance of that name. Basically, there is no *xenos*, there is no foreigner before or outside the *xenia*, this pact or exchange with a group. Or to be more precise, with a line of descent [...] And the same word is translated in two ways, sometimes by *étranger* [stranger or foreigner], sometimes by *hôte* [host]. That is understandable, no doubt. It reminds us of or intimates the necessity of a passage in culture, between the two meanings of the word *xenos*, but strictly speaking it remains hard to justify.[10]

In this way, where Dupont, the anthropologist of the ancient world, sees a translation error and an essentialisation of descriptive relational terms, Derrida, the philosopher, focuses on the difficulty involved in the same word switching from one meaning to another, while still acknowledging the necessity of finding this 'passage in culture'. However, as we shall see a little later, the anthropological description focuses precisely on the question of how the stranger can be made a guest in accordance with the cultural codes of the societies that offer him or her a welcome. It might be supposed that it would be enough to respond *in situ*, as Dupont does when, refuting any essentialism, she suggests conducting empirical investigations based on historical situations. But that will not prevent the existence of the definition that Derrida is anxious to retain, that of the absolute and sacred stranger, a definition that means that hospitality is regarded as an unconditional virtue and is imperative because of the absolute nature of this figure of the stranger. It is this injunction, powerful yet at the same time fragile, that we need to understand.

A useful starting point would be the compatibility between Derrida's decontextualized vision of hospitality and the religious notion of the sacred. In the course of a symposium organised in the late 1990s by social workers who urged the philosopher to expand on his vision of unconditional welcome and on the notion of the stranger, Derrida responded as follows:

> Within the hypothesis of pure hospitality, I want to offer my house, my home, my language, my nation, but I must offer beyond what I can give to someone who is absolutely other and without any limits. Hospitality either must be unconditional and without any limits or is neither of these. While there is no particular need to add a theological dimension to all of that, the possibility nevertheless remains that such an approach will lead to a theology as long as hospitality is imbued with a sacred character and associated with religiosity (as opposed to positive religion). When we say to someone who has just arrived 'make yourself at home', there is something religious, something sacred, something associated with the infinite about the words. They are indeed strong words, but they should nevertheless not be avoided.[11]

How, then, can we approach in practical terms this absolute hospitality, stripped as it is of any context and universal in nature, when it struggles to descend from that pure heaven of beliefs and of virtues where the very people who are in favour of it (philosophers, believers, activists) also want to confine it? We need to topple the statue from its pedestal and strip it of its inhuman superiority, yet without shattering it into pieces. Another philosopher, René Scherer, author of a key work entitled *Zeus hospitalier*, provides us with some guidance when proposing a reading of the mythical tale of the *Odyssey*. He writes:

> Let us open the *Odyssey* at the verses describing the final return of Ulysses to Ithaca. In order to prevent his being recognised, Athena ages him and disguises him as a beggar – no doubt to ensure that his appearance would be as far removed as possible from that of the glorious hero everyone is expecting, but also (we cannot help thinking) in order that the test of hospitality towards the lowliest and most rejected should be complete. And she succeeds in Ulysses's very first encounter, with the swineherd Eumaeus, who is himself an inferior being. When Ulysses thanks him for welcoming him so sincerely in spite of his rags, Eumaeus replies: 'Rudeness to a stranger is not decency, poor though he may be, poorer than you. All wanderers and beggars come from Zeus. What we can give is slight but well-meant – all we dare.'[12]

A few pages earlier, the same Schérer mentions Plato, who is preoccupied above all with the laws of the city. And Plato invites us to contextualise and politicise the gesture made by Eumaeus, the welcoming swineherd. For Plato, of all the obligations imposed on citizens, hospitality is the most important one. It is a 'sacred duty' that cannot be infringed without exposure to the punishment of the gods. The latter are particularly attentive to the protection of strangers and foreigners, since, as Plato writes, 'the foreigner is not surrounded by friends and companions and stirs the compassion of gods and men that much more' – and in particular that of the supreme god, hospitable Zeus.[13]

So, as we see, both Homer and Plato refer to family and friends, to laws and customs, to obligations and respect, and the reader discovers the relationships and social rules that form the basis of what might be called the rationale of hospitality. Of course, there are always gods everywhere, ready to see to the opening of the door, to ensuring the encounter takes place, to making sure someone gets in somewhere. In religions based on polytheism and animism, we often find, on thresholds, these tutelary divinities who intervene in human matters, facilitating journeys and instigating relationships – the Eshu or Exú among the Yoruba people or in the Brazilian Candomblé, Legba in voodoo rituals.

Guillaume Le Blanc, another philosopher, turns his attention to the political dimension of this hospitality imposed on us by the gods. For him, this stranger, protected and introduced by the gods, embodies the essence of vulnerability.[14] The relationship with the gods and the relationship with vulnerability go hand in hand and are intertwined, and this double relationship allows the absolute beneficiary of hospitality to be identified and enables us to understand what the concept of universal hospitality means: hospitality as a duty of care towards those who are most 'vulnerable' would be an 'infrapolitics of subaltern lives'.[15] But is this really a matter of 'infrapolitics'? Are we not already, quite simply, in the political domain? For the protagonist of hospitality here is the stranger, a person stripped bare and cast out from society, physically and socially destitute, someone whose vulnerability (which must be cared for) is associated with an absence of place or of recognition in the political world. It is therefore not only in obedience to civil law but also in our own interests that we conform to the principles of hospitality; for, as Plato said, 'practically all offenses committed as between or against foreigners are quicker to attract the vengeance of God than offences as between fellow citizens'.[16] In the political language of today, this is a matter of correcting the imperfect Athenian democracy. For either strangers are destitute and are not citizens, or else they are naked because they are not citizens. The naked human is closer to god than the citizen; the latter must therefore consult the god in order to be able to identify, with his help, who should benefit from hospitality.

We are already in the domain of anthropology here, an anthropology of social and political life where hospitality is part of a cycle, or at least part of an exchange mechanism (but, we may well ask, what are the limits of this exchange mechanism today?). Moreover, for Benveniste, hospitality 'is illuminated by reference to potlatch, of which it is a weakened form'.[17] On the other hand, apparently in complete contrast with this notion, Derrida sees in the 'logic of the gift' something 'terrifying', the sign of a suspect generosity. 'As for the gift and the counter-gift', he says, 'the exchange system does not belong in the domain of hospitality. Pure hospitality is a gift that cannot be exchanged without any consideration of reward.'[18] This law, he adds, does not exist in any legislation as a social, political, legal, or economic norm or prescription. Always asocial, apolitical, and outside economic considerations, it is by nature transgressive. It could be said that it exists solely to trigger personal sacrifice and a stripping away of the self in order to give some meaning to our temporary renunciation of some part of the space, time, or money for the benefit of the guest we have welcomed in. These are transgressive values that can be embodied in the practices associated with hospitality, with the risk that this might entail breaking the law, or something close to that. 'We are not urging civil disobedience as such, nor are we inviting anyone to disobey the law, but we are saying that a given law, in the name of another higher law, is a bad one.'[19]

Derrida was undoubtedly right to insist. At the very least, it is possible to acknowledge, with him, that unconditional hospitality still exists. He too wanted to bring about this transition, which goes from stranger to guest, even if 'that remains difficult to justify'.[20] I would like to look in more depth at this train of thought, of investigation, and potentially of action, without however abandoning the criticism of essentialist or ontological interpretations of the stranger and of his or her host implicit in the repeated assertions made by the philosopher, as discussed above; or, more precisely, I would like to restore these injunctions and these beliefs to their proper place, given the fact that they do indeed exist in our societies.

The argument that Derrida develops in the course of various texts and public debates dates from the mid-1990s. In a context marked by the movements of population provoked by major crises in the Balkans or in the African Great Lakes region, his argument was part of a body of sociological research and philosophical essays devoted to the issue of refugees and their treatment. In 1995 the International Parliament of Writers launched the Charter of Cities of Asylum, reinforced that same year by the creation of a network of asylum cities and then further strengthened, the following year, by the First Congress of Cities of Asylum, which had the aim of welcoming writers, artists or intellectuals who faced persecution in their native countries. Such initiatives did not spread on the scale expected. Yet, twenty years later, they are still there, their ambitions broadened to encompass all exiles, migrants, and asylum seekers in Europe – in the form of demonstrations of commitment on behalf of municipal councillors from within the network of host cities or in the manifesto of refuge cities ('We, the cities of Europe') signed by several mayors of major European cities including Ada Colau for Barcelona, or Anne Hidalgo for Paris. The mayors of Lampedusa, of Palermo, of Madrid and many other cities have also declared their readiness to offer hospitality.

It was on the occasion of the First Congress of the Cities of Asylum in 1996, which Derrida was unable to attend in person, that his text, published the following year under the title *Cosmopolitans of the World, Unite!*, was read out for the first time. For him, as we have seen, hospitality is unconditional and the stranger is an absolute concept, which can be defined only in the absence of any context. Seen in a concrete and pragmatic way, this position is challenging: if I do not welcome into my home anyone who turns up, I am going against the ethics of hospitality, even though I admire its beauty and its grandeur. Moreover, the implications of this position extend well beyond my own personal moral coherence, in that, if all the inhabitants of my building, my area, or my village do not feel under an obligation to respect the duty of hospitality, just what and whom is it supposed to serve? How far can its implementation be pushed back and, conversely, what effect do such practical results have on its principles and on the moral injunction itself?

The question that the anthropologist must therefore ask concerns what is to be done with this concept of unconditional hospitality and where it should be made to sit within a social and political anthropology of hospitality. There is no need to be prescriptive about all this – it is simply a matter of looking further afield.

The elementary forms of hospitality

The philosopher's problem is that, all too often, he or she sets out the ethics of a situation without paying attention to real life, whereas in fact ethics refers to the everyday reality of the difficult choices each of us is obliged to make. In this precise case, the philosopher advocates values and invokes unwritten laws without, in doing so, taking into consideration the relative and relational nature of the social contexts in which they are to be implemented. Setting ethical necessity over any other eventuality, he or she makes a moral point (both on an individual and on a collective scale) out of a question that is essentially social, cultural, and political: the relationship between global mobility and local attachment. Regularly invoked by those defending the cause of undocumented individuals, of migrants or of refugees, Derrida's argument has attracted criticism from those who specialise in moral and political philosophy. Thus Magali Bessone condemns and deconstructs this 'ethicization' of the migrant question and the public and media uses of the 'hospitality metaphor'.[21] Similarly, for Benjamin Boudou, if on the one hand the rhetoric of hospitality opens up 'a critical grammar of repressive laws against migrants', on the other hand 'there is nothing obvious in having recourse to a practice and an idea as anachronistic as hospitality', at the risk of 'moralising law and politics'.[22]

How is it possible to talk about hospitality today without falling into the traps of either sanctification or rejection, both in the social context and in that of individual ethics and of politics? Anthropologists take a very different approach from that of philosophers and, if they encounter the questions raised by the latter, it is because they come across them in the 'field', through shared experiences, and by putting moral values back into the context in which they were stated, in other words within their conditions of possibility. They are interested in the elementary forms of hospitality, a new point of departure for the debate. In answer to the question 'Whom am I willing or obliged to welcome into my home?', each person tends to provide an answer that is as absolute as the unconditional hospitality exhorted by Derrida: in the private world of welcome, I invite into my home whomever I choose, guided by a 'predisposition of the individual spirit' and by an availability that, in the context of love or of a gift given freely and in the absence of any kind of calculation or expectation, can even amount to a 'hospitality without limits',[23] outside any normative reference. But then, thus determined by his or her own unconditional desire, the host will set about curbing the extent of his or her gesture by demarcating what is involved: I welcome into my home whomever I choose, in other words parents, children, friends, and lovers. I extend a welcome to cousins, an uncle, perhaps an aunt, unless I do not get along with her. For this definition is not purely family-oriented. In the actual experience of hospitality, there is indeed a 'practical kinship' as opposed to a 'kinship that is put on display', just as Pierre Bourdieu observed in his study of Kabyle families.[24] Throughout the network of relationships that acts, at one and the same time, as an asset and as a constraint, there are people we get on with and with whom we do indeed live, work or cohabit. But, just as relationships go beyond kinship and the domestic world, the domain of hospitality extends in the same way, and the 'familiar' is not limited only to the 'familial'. There are still elements of the familiar in the spheres of trust with which we surround ourselves: in the voluntary sector, in the field of religion, in that of politics, and anywhere where people can be grouped by network, relationships, trust, shared beliefs, and so on, moving within different relational worlds.

From an ethnographic point of view, unconditional hospitality does not disappear, but its expression and its implementation need to be contextualised. For Julian Pitt-Rivers, an anthropologist specialising in Andalucía and author of a famous essay on the law of hospitality, hospitality stems 'not from divine revelation [...] but from sociological necessity'.[25] It is this latter, in contrast to the definition championed by Derrida, that is the general law, abstract and natural, and that places hospitality within the reciprocity of relationships between individuals or groups: 'The law of hospitality is founded upon ambivalence', Pitt-Rivers observes. 'It imposes order through an appeal to the sacred, makes the unknown knowable, and replaces conflict by reciprocal honour.'[26] In these conditions, the universal is not to be found in the sacred – the latter can vary depending on the specific cultures within which the different 'codes of hospitality' are expressed – but rather in the relational laws that enable the reciprocal challenge of hospitality to be successfully overcome. So, writes Pitt-Rivers,

> Convention demands that each foreigner be made a guest in Andalucía. The unincorporated stranger cannot be abided. The plebeian etiquette with regard to eating illustrates this general sentiment. The act of eating supposes a higher degree of intimacy than mere presence and to eat in front of a stranger is to offend this sentiment. His status must be changed therefore to that of guest and this is done by the formality of offering food.[27]

In this reciprocal ordeal, there is a symmetry of obligations and at the same time a dissymmetry of status between the guest and the head of the household. And if the individual alone turns out to be unable to deal with the situation, then the relationship of reciprocity is transferred to his or her community. From hospitality in the strictest sense we shift to an extended form of hospitality.

We are back to the potlatch referred to by Benveniste, albeit deployed in a somewhat disillusioned way. For the sense of honour runs extremely deep here and, as a result, this symbolic retribution for the partner in the relationship can never be treated lightly. In the same way, it is impossible for the person who offers and for the one who receives hospitality to be equal *at the same moment in time*. Finally, the element of hostility that constitutes part of the condition (and of the name) of the guest[28] disappears only once the test of hospitality is over, when the foreigner 'forfeits his association with the sacred and his call upon hospitality which derived from it'.[29] Such are the laws of hospitality, a fragile relationship which relies on the complementarity of roles and foresees its own demise – in the form of social integration, inclusion, or otherwise in departure, rejection or abandonment.

As the sociologist Anne Gotman demonstrates following the joint research projects she coordinated in France during the 1990s, hospitality has a beginning and an end and entails a time and a space of waiting, a provisional condition.[30] Similarly, *xenia* in ancient Greece also implies that the guest is 'always on the point of leaving': 'Everything is done to ensure that the welcome extended to the stranger is for a specific period; in fact, it rarely lasts more than three days.'[31] And in Homer, too, the welcome Ulysses receives at each stage of his odyssey takes more or less the same ritual form from one place to the next, a form that ends with the guest's departure: the welcome meal, the bath, the traveller's account of his voyage, the feast, the preparation of the stranger's bed, usually in the entrance hall, the parting gifts.[32]

Whether in the form of hospitality, 'receiving' the stranger, or 'returning' the invitation, hospitality is always a relationship. Never without conditions, it is a way of recognising the Other, but in a concrete way, just as he or she presents themselves, and of giving them a place within a space. It is at this point that hospitality becomes a subject for anthropology. The person who is received 'steps ipso facto into the spiral of debt'.[33] Hospitality is the beginning of a 'series of obligations', as Anne Gotman reiterates, a commitment to a relationship. It needs to be studied in all its conditions, but also in all its forms: it is a gift of space, of time, and of money.

By proceeding through a series of concentric circles, of networks, and of usages until it becomes possible to identify the tipping point, the dilution, or the disappearance of hospitality in areas where it is no longer appropriate, it is possible to avoid, or at any rate to keep at bay, the trap of a metaphorical use of the concept. The starting point will therefore be hospitality in its strictest sense, in the domestic context, and one perceived as being 'by definition clandestine [...] the obsession of modern states',[34] since the private sphere still remains outside their control. Yet the very thing that defines hospitality, at that particular moment, in opposition to the state – the 'I can welcome into my home whomever I like' – can be turned on its head and immediately creates a condition, my personal good will. Hospitality, in its initial expression, is not unconditional or absolute but conditional, relational, and contextual. The family, generally relatively small in size, or expanding but not excessively, becomes the context in which a relationship is established with the guest. How does hospitality become part of an exchange? It is first of all a practical question, in that it entails having space in a physical sense, and also making space in a social sense. The forms and the meaning of hospitality are expanding for practical reasons and according to certain social rules.

In order to clarify this, I would like to refer to some research that I carried out in West Africa, among Hausa migrants and traders, or involving people said to be Hausa or whose common language and principal social codes are Hausa, even though they come from at least twenty different (albeit neighbouring) ethnic identities. From North Nigeria and Niger, they have spread throughout all of West Africa (to the south of Nigeria, in Benin, Togo, Ghana) where they set up settlements called *zongo* for foreigners.

The *mai gida* – important figures, landlords, and heads of these commercial networks – welcome strangers into their homes. They do so first of all in the name of *sadaka*, literally a form of alms, the impersonal gift to God, and we therefore find here, in a precise context, the implementation of an unconditional hospitality in its sacred dimension. It is a propitiatory ritual, a sacrifice of material goods in exchange for a symbolic benefit like those generally observed in the religious practice of charity. In his book *The Gift: The Form and Reason for Exchange in Archaic Societies*, the anthropologist Marcel Mauss devoted a short paragraph to the Hausas' *sadaka*. For him, the institution of *sadaka* is both a sacrificial rite and a gift. And he explains:

> Generosity is an obligation, because Nemesis avenges the poor and the gods for the superabundance of happiness and wealth of certain people who should rid themselves of it. This is the ancient morality of the gift, which has become a principle of justice. The gods and the spirits accept that the share of wealth and happiness that has been offered to them and had been hitherto destroyed in useless sacrifices should serve the poor and children.[35]

By offering *sadaka*, the *mai gida* can, by the same token, increase their 'wealth in men' (*arzikin mutane*). Therefore *sadaka*, a virtue, an unconditional gift, is not given entirely freely. The gesture of welcome is linked to a desire for symbolic prestige, and also for 'social capital', to return to the concept outlined by Bourdieu. The *mai gida* have at the same time the role of heads of family, of important traders, and of landlords. They are described as *mai karban baki*, 'those who take in strangers'. Yet, as in the research undertaken by Pitt-Rivers in Andalucía or by Anne Gotman in Paris and the Paris Region [Île de France], the relationship that is set in place at such a time is a hierarchical one. It is a reciprocal and asymmetrical relationship. Even if the person being welcomed is an adult, that person will be referred to as *yaro*, 'child' and will take on that status. The *yaro* is available, he works for his *mai gida* when required to do so. And the latter has a duty to protect 'his' or 'her' stranger. The expression 'my stranger' is one frequently heard in Africa. When someone is given a particularly warm welcome, the person who acts as host will say: 'You have nothing to be afraid of. You are *my stranger*.'

A song sung by the children from the Koranic school in the Zongo district – the Hausa district in Lomé, where I conducted this research – highlights in just a few words the protocol for hospitality that is practiced there: 'If a stranger comes to your house, he will say: "Excuse me". And you will reply: "Be welcome, stranger, son of my mother". You will offer him a place to sit down and you will give him water, and then you will talk to him and there will be friendly conversation.' This song refers to the 'son of my mother' (*dan uwanci*). This term evokes a kinship on the maternal side, but is also used to refer to relationships in a broader sense, and thus to 'kinship' in an indeterminate way. It means that I treat the stranger as my kin and that I speak to him or her in a friendly manner. More often, the relationship between the guest and the host is portrayed by the word *zumunci*, a challenging word to translate and for which different writers have come up with a range of options such as affectivity, alliance, sense of clan, relationship with a person from the same country, mutual understanding, or, finally (and most accurately in the light of my own observations), quasi-kinship.[36] But, to qualify a little further what the children from the Koranic school in the neighbourhood were singing, the relationship of *zumunci* is not necessarily an emotional one. As René Schérer says on the subject of the emotions associated with hospitality, what is needed is friendship, but not too much of it. This relationship corresponds to a situation where the individuals concerned cannot be entirely sure whether they are the target of hospitality or of hostility. The one does not completely erase the other. Instead it is an intermediate state, and the *zumunci* establishes itself in a practical form in places that occupy a peripheral or marginal space in the residential quarters of the *mai gida*, thus allowing a certain amount of reserve to be exercised on both sides. Two people who can claim to have *zumunci* between them are not necessarily friends. But a hostile gesture (a theft for example, committed by the *yaro* in the host's home) will instantly destroy the trust (*amana*), which must prevail in the relationship and which constitutes its only guarantee.

Subsequently, after a few days or a few years, the relationship comes to an end and the stranger who has been made welcome by his *mai gida* can either begin to work regularly within the landlord's circle of dependants, or else leave in order to resume his journey, unless that is, he decides to begin trading on his own account, generally with the help of the *mai gida*. It can also happen – and this is the ideal outcome, the dream of every *yaro* – that the relationship between them changes its nature and the stranger becomes *suruki*, 'son-in-law', as a result of being given a wife from within the family or from the immediate circle of the *mai gida*. At such a time there is no longer any *zumunci* between them, and a form of social integration within the town is established. In this sense, the *zumunci* is not just a relationship between two individuals, the stranger and the host, but refers back to a community institution intended to reinforce the social order, the social world of the Hausas in Lomé and in coastal towns of the Gulf of Guinea in general. By integrating migrants into an extended family, Hausa traders enhance their own capacity to become part of a town or a region where their community is a minority and where, even if many have been naturalised, they are collectively regarded as strangers. Saying 'so and so, this stranger, is my child, he lives in my house, I protect him' also means expanding the extent of their own social influence as a result of the control exerted by the assimilation of new arrivals.

Each culture can have its own language of hospitality. However, beyond certain local cultural and linguistic particularities, the case of the Hausas is an illustration of a number of fundamental rules that can be seen elsewhere. Thus, as Anne Gotman points out, in the relationship involved in hospitality there is indeed asymmetry rather than equality.[37] But this inequality does not prevent reciprocity. Similarly, Julian Pitt-Rivers highlights the fragility of the relationship between guest and host: 'While it lasts,' he writes, 'the tenuous nature of the relationship of host and guest depends upon respecting the complementarity of their roles.'[38] This asymmetry entails an exchange, and hospitality sets in place a cycle of gifts and counter-gifts demarcated by a beginning and an end. This end occurs either when the guest is fully integrated or when he or she ceases to accept this asymmetric relationship: 'Thus while the mode of permanent incorporation solidifies in time, the status of guest evaporates',[39] adds Pitt-Rivers. Indeed, the duration of hospitality varies in length and, meanwhile, the relationship is always in suspension: in the case of the Hausas of Lomé, for example, it can last for a period of three days, as in ancient Greece (rarely more than three days, according to Dupont), and this length of time is also the reference point for good practice in hospitality among the Hazaras of Afghanistan, where, furthermore, a guest room is kept available close to the entrance of the house.[40] However, in the Zongo district of Lomé, the *yaro* could stay with the *mai gida* much longer than three days, extending his stay to months, even years. In any case, as long as the *yaro* remains a guest, 'his coming does not stop:

he continues to come', he 'remains a stranger'.[41] This extended duration can be linked to the social organisation, which regards the free movement of foreigners as essential.

The happy outcome of the Hausas' hospitality, when the host presents the 'child', *yaro* – with a bride, raises a fundamental question. Apart from providing insight into the temporal limits of the welcome and into the foreseeable transformations of the always provisional status of the guest, this outcome also touches on the potential role hospitality can play in the intimate lives of the stranger and of his landlord. This dimension inevitably conjures up an imaginary realm embellished with tales of exotic customs, recounted with varying degrees of reliability, which I must mention before going any further. Such tales include reference to the much famed hospitality with sexual gratification – a 'tradition' often evoked in connection with the Inuit; but also worth mentioning is the 'wedding of Attila', king of the Huns whose hospitality within his castle was as renowned as his cruelty outside its walls. On the banks of the Danube, the hospitality ceremony performed for the envoys of Roman emperors included presents before their departure, the provision of meals, and, 'in the case of the overnight stay of Roman guests [...] the traditional custom of providing beautiful young girls for their pleasure'.[42] Unusual on account of the quality of the guests mentioned (in this case ambassadors) and on account of the empirical evidence provided, this practice, in the context of the Inuit, was a source of much fascination to twentieth-century explorers, who, it would appear, considerably exaggerated the role of this sexual gratification in the system of hospitality. Few investigations have been carried out on the subject apart from one by Bernard Saladin d'Anglure. The latter approaches the matter in conjunction with another question, notably that of adoption, which indeed constitutes a far more widespread and well-confirmed practice.

> If there is one characteristic of the Inuit population that has particularly struck the imagination of western observers – alongside exotic practices like the consumption of raw meats, the use of snow houses, the exchange of spouses or hospitality with sexual gratification, a practice that has been exaggerated in the European imagination in a manner that has little to do with the indeed rather limited experience of the few travellers who reported it – it is indeed the importance of adoption, mentioned in travel accounts from the beginning of the nineteenth century, when the first contacts with the Canadian Central Arctic occurred.[43]

In fact there is every indication that the 'sexual gratification' of the guest is only very peripherally connected to other, more developed practices in Inuit society that bring a certain 'fluidity' to the rules governing marriage and filiation. These practices include the exchange of spouses in the context of marriage and the ritual role of godparents, or the use of adoption in that of filiation. These are, according to the ethnologist, ways of maintaining social cohesion and a collective approach to the dangers that individualism might represent to the survival of members of a community faced with particularly challenging conditions of existence. Following the same principle, at the heart of the group, 'Inuit practices of hospitality guarantee that anyone who does not have enough food has the right to enter the homes of those who do and eat', observes Bernard Saladin d'Anglure.

With reference to adoption in particular, this practice in fact involves the circulation of children in a social organisation that functions beyond the simple domestic context. Saladin refers to what he calls 'transfer', whereas earlier researchers tended to use the term 'adoption'. The hypothesis of a demographic redistribution and of an economic balance, although not the only one to examine here, should be considered, insofar as the 'gift' of newborn or yet to be born children enables the composition of families to be restored to balance according to resources and needs. In real terms, within the adoptive home, the child – given by another family in the kinship, or else an orphan – takes the place of a dead member, whether child or adult, whose name he or she will also take. Symbolically, adoption is associated with female sterility, which can be resolved only through shamanic intervention, by allowing the woman in question to go 'in quest of' a child (a 'baby from the earth') in the realm of myths. This is why children who are passed on form part of the kinship – but not in a complete sense, for they are still 'sent' by shamans, even if in reality they come from relatives or friends. There, too, a spiritual dimension underpins the unquestionable and 'absolute' nature of the reality of taking in a child from outside the home, even though, for the anthropologist, this divine injunction can be understood only insofar as it is the best possible application of a sociological rule.

This is what Saladin demonstrates by situating adoptions within the context of 'social transfers of human life' that enable the reproduction of the group (adopted children represent about a third of the total number of children). His argument is that such transfers contribute to the fluidity of Inuit society as a whole. In the same vein, there are also 'all kinds of transfers, whether migratory movement between local or regional groups, high rates of adoption, systematic sharing of goods or exchanges of spouses, not to mention the consumption of food during visits or by visitors'. He compares this type of social organisation with the sedentary and proprietorial relationships in western societies, which are taken as the model by anthropologists who cannot fail to observe, at the very least, 'the impression of flexibility' that they find in Inuit societies. In contrast, Saladin draws attention to the 'overlapping' of social frameworks that result from these 'transfers', in particular in the case of adoption (which causes at least two families to 'overlap'). More generally, it is a matter of understanding society from the standpoint of these 'overlap' situations, formed by the multiple points of anchorage of different individuals, rather than from the standpoint, generally favoured by observers, of fixed social units (on a domestic or larger scale). If we look in this way at society as a whole (vertical intergenerational overlappings or horizontal ones between families and households), adoption plays a central rather than a marginal role, alongside other transfers or movements.

Here we are faced with a question that directly concerns the link between nomads, strangers, those 'on the move' in a general sense, and the sedentary social form of the house, *domus*. The issue of the Inuit 'nomadic children' can be set alongside that of the 'child circulation' among the working-class populations of Brazil.[44] The latter is not, strictly speaking, a form of adoption but rather a matter of finding 'placements' for children. As in the case of hospitality, it involves the child being welcomed into another house and given shelter. There is also sometimes, in certain houses, the issue of children working, and there is systematically a language of quasi-kinship that allows people who do not necessarily have close links to be brought together in a social context. Just as, in the Catholic religion, godparents pledge to offer a spiritual relationship, a similar phenomenon happens within metaphorical kinship: we refer to an uncle as an 'honorary father' (*pai de consideraçâo*) and use the term 'honorary uncle' (*tio de consideraçâo*) for someone who is close but unrelated. In this case, among urban Brazilians, the host families have a social status marginally superior to that of the children's original families, and a link – through

kinship, through religion, or through a local neighbourhood – must always exist in order to guarantee
the welcome and the 'upbringing' of the child over a
period of several years, with complete confidence on
both sides.

So why this detour through practices of adoption in
the Canadian Arctic and in the working-class urban
population of Brazil? Because from the moment any
reference is made to the 'archaic' and 'exotic' nature of
a hospitality whose real social forms were disappearing
at the very moment the word was coming back into
use in our globalised twenty-first-century societies, it
is interesting to understand the social logics and the
symbolic dimensions associated with this practice. Both
adoption and hospitality involve welcoming into our
home someone who is from outside the family, an act
that entails finding a space within a zone where the
inside and the outside 'overlap'. Yet the examples given
here show that the link between the two practices is
not confined to this analogy: chronologically, hospitality can be seen as being in some way the condition
and the practical implementation of adoption. The
two eventually come together by creating, at the very
heart of societies, channels or the social network of
an opening, in the form of the welcome and the space
offered to those in transit (children, migrants); and
that opening is then extended, or likely to be extended,
in an intricate and interconnected way, towards the
boundaries of society and beyond.

The social does not, however, preclude the private or
the intimate. In accounts of hospitality we find many
references to a 'gift of self' and to love, which the
philosopher René Schérer illustrates by reminding us of
the feelings experienced by the three successive hostesses
of Ulysses – Calypso, Circe, and Nausicaa – notably the
seduction of the moment of encounter, the desire for a
lasting union, and the subsequent heartbreak provoked

by the stranger's departure. If such feelings can be kindled by the gestures of contemporary hospitality in the same way as filial sentiments sometimes are, or those that find in sponsorship the ritual expression of a personalised support for young migrants, it would be interesting to resituate them and to understand them in contexts where these practices play, or have played, a central role in social regulation.

From domestic hospitality to public hospitality

In order to further explore this anthropology of a possible and worthy hospitality, in other words, one that is effective without necessarily being 'gentle and kind', we must now look at the expansion of the practices of hospitality. This will entail a change of scale and will take us to a zone of superimposition, and even of confusion, between the form of hospitality that we have been focusing on – that is, private or limited hospitality (one confined to an inter-individual relationship between landlords and 'their' strangers) – and an expanded version of hospitality. This 'zone' where restricted–expanded or private–public overlap can be approached in two ways, namely from an anthropological and from a historical perspective.

From an anthropological point of view, if I go back to my own West African field of research, I notice that *zumunci*, the term used to describe the relationship of hospitality among Hausa foreigners from the coastal towns, is also the name given to a support organisation providing help not only for its needy members, but also for strangers and foreigners in need of support. With this in mind, household chiefs, traders, and neighbourhood dignitaries save money in order to redistribute it in the name of the *sadaqah*, the Muslim tradition of giving alms or charity (the same religious terms justifies welcoming the stranger into one's home, as has been pointed out). The accounts of the Zumunci Club cover two main categories. One is designed to support the inhabitants of the Zongo district, in other words oriented towards an immediate sphere of mutual acquaintances and networks associated with the *mai gida* who are members of the organisation. The other is for beggars, wanderers, strangers, and anyone without solid and permanent connections to the community of the Zongo district. In this way the Zumunci Club fulfils a role of mediation, expanding the mutual obligations of the people of Zongo to a more distant circle, through a solidarity that is increasingly 'public' and anonymous.

Generally speaking, in any community-based organisation, whether religious, political, or local, the guest can be someone I do not know, but he or she will be rendered more familiar or less of a stranger through the existence of a link that is sufficiently strong to ensure a welcome. Where domestic and public hospitality are superimposed, the outsider can become part of a network. In such a case, the individual is neither too socially isolated nor integrated in a too rigid social structure, but is somewhere between the two: he or she can create a sense of family in a social network that extends beyond the family, for example in the fabric of the community. From this point of view, religious organisations are important in that they provide a context that is almost family-like by extending private hospitality to structures which are further and further removed from the family. Take also the partisan welcome extended in France to Chilean, Argentinian, or Brazilian exiles in the 1970s. Even though the host and the guest did not know each other, a relationship of sufficient trust was nevertheless established through the medium of political solidarity.

This change of scale can therefore be analysed by anthropology from the perspective of social structures:

hospitality takes place in a succession of networks – first- and second-order stars, as British anthropologists described the sociography of networks – the links developing from one person to another, in an unbroken chain.[45] In this case, hospitality *is* sociability within a social milieu that, both structurally and circumstantially, makes room for the stranger. This social organisation has a key influence on the encounter and the relative proximity between the host who extends a welcome and the outsider who is welcomed. The tipping point remains to be determined between a social form that could be described as family-oriented or based on the immediate or on the larger scale community and an anonymous link. The ramification of networks gives rise to the formation of a border between the inside and the outside, between what relates to hospitality in the strictest sense and is always offered within the context of a relationship, and something else, which is more distant, without necessarily being a separate entity. In many languages the same word is used for both guest and host, the two forming a mirror image of each other. The relationship between these two people is the condition *sine qua non* of hospitality. It is delegated only when it is no longer possible to be absolutely certain about the context and the relationship in which the welcome will take place. But the word is still present. At that point hospitality will be referred to in a broader and then 'public' sense, in the context of a 'policy of hospitality', and its meaning will be increasingly metaphorical.

Historically, what is generally referred to as 'public' hospitality goes back to the towns of the Middle Ages, with their establishment of hospices or alms houses and the expansion of charitable work within the church. Certain writers regard these institutions as the historical origins of humanitarian action. But they are also the arena of the first political controls enforced on the destitute. The role of provider of hospitality was

delegated to the church and, gradually, to public institutions. From that point on we move away from the
fundamentally anthropological relationship of gift and
counter-gift, which established hospitality as a form of
exchange. But all this gives us grounds for reflection that
we can bear in mind when considering this particular
manifestation of the expansion of hospitality, which
takes the form of hospitality on a community scale.

A long historical tracking shot allows us to see
how, in the nineteenth and twentieth centuries, public
hospitality becomes a matter for states and in so doing
disappears, to be replaced by asylum and refugee rights.
The nation-state has assumed responsibility for asylum
but has integrated this right of asylum into policies of
border controls of territories and free movement. The
word 'asylum' is still used in a double sense: that of
giving asylum and that of locking someone away in
an asylum. Within this terminology and within these
policies, all trace of hospitality has been lost. Hence
the point of view, expressed by the most critical writers
today, that the very idea of public hospitality is a
deceptive metaphor for national integration policies
while in reality referring to immigration controls.
Thus, for Sophie Djigo, philosopher and author of a
study on migrants in Calais, the hospitality analogy
is fallacious insofar as it is based on the notion of 'a
national "home" seen as simply the plural version of
an "individual home"'.[46] As a result, the fantasy of a
'national house'[47] begins to take shape along the lines
proposed by the philosopher Wendy Brown: those of
a strong state needing to protect the fragile nation.[48]
Strictly speaking, this principle of public or state hospitality, sometimes demanded by citizens who support a
more dignified and humane treatment of migrants on
the part of their government, is compatible with the
sedentary and proprietorial conception of the social
organisation: the owners of the national house welcome

into their home whomever they choose, will open their doors, or else erect walls according to their personal decision, their own goodwill.

Yet, in spite of all this, hospitality is still present – in the form of an idea, a word, an archaic or exotic vestige, but also in individual or collective initiatives that imply a criticism of public policies, with their sense of fear and reticence towards the integration of certain strangers, and that seek instead an alternative solution. A history of hospitality therefore extends into the present and is unfolding right in front of our eyes but in a constant state of transformation. What, then, is being done today *in the name of* hospitality?

2

Hospitality

The Challenge of the Present

An account of actions that demonstrate support for the welcome of migrants points to an evolution at the heart of European societies in the twenty-first century. The sheer extent of these actions and the sense of commitment that underpins them, as well as the forms of solidarity and of hospitality involved, increasingly begin to resemble a social movement. On 4 January 2017, Cédric Herrou, a farmer from the Roya Valley, near the Italian border, appeared in court in Nice. Eight months later, he received a four-month suspended sentence for aiding illegal immigrants. It was an 'honour' to have done so, he said, adding that his actions were 'political'. A hundred or so migrants were being housed with local people in the Roya Valley at that time. Arriving at the border on foot, they were welcomed and given food and accommodation by some of the local inhabitants. In September 2017, the teacher and researcher Pierre-Alain Mannoni was accused of 'assisting illegal entry and free movement of unauthorized persons' and, after almost one year of legal proceedings, was given a two-month suspended sentence. As in the case of Cédric

Herrou, the sentences handed down on appeal were more severe than the initial judgement.

Also in 2017, a local organization was set up in the Briançon area to provide help and accommodation for migrants who had lost their way in the mountains after illegally crossing the Franco-Italian border at Col de l'Échelle, at an altitude of 1,700 meters. On an almost daily basis, people familiar with the mountains, including mountain and walking guides or ski patrols, organized search parties to rescue walkers who had got into difficulties, just as sailors would go to the aid of any vessel in distress. Their actions were, of course, 'unconditional' – that is, not dependent in any way on the legal status of the individual at the moment of rescue. In Barcelonnette, a mountain village of just over 2,000 inhabitants in the nearby region of Alpes-de-Haute-Provence, the arrival of migrants in 2016 and the welcome extended to them led to unprecedented levels of involvement, giving rise to a community of local solidarity that had hitherto been dormant, and this commitment brought with it an 'emotional overin-vestment' on the part of those involved, a predominantly female solidarity network. Generally speaking, local networks such as these have played a key role in organizing accommodation for migrants. Examples like these are commonplace and occur in many different places throughout Europe.

On 18 February 2017, 160,000 people marched through the streets of Barcelona alongside the mayor of the city, Ada Colau, to demonstrate their support for the welcome of migrants and refugees and to show their opposition to the Spanish government, which had initially committed to taking in 16,000 people, in accordance with the European agreement of September 2015, an agreement that made provision for the relocation of 160,000 refugees across the whole of Europe. A year and a half later, Spain had in fact taken in only 1,000. And in most other European countries this announcement, made by the various governments, had produced little or no impact. Then, in September 2017, the programme set up by the European Commission to relocate asylum seekers and refugees was officially abandoned, with less than a third of the commitments undertaken by European governments honoured.

Elsewhere, for example in the north of France in the aftermath of the demolition of the Calais shanty town in October 2016, or in Paris after the evacuation of makeshift campsites during the same year, people joined forces to open their own homes to asylum seekers, for a limited period and within the protective context of an organization. Their aim, as they explained on social media, was to put pressure on the state, which was failing to respect the legal obligation to provide shelter for asylum seekers.

What does a closer examination of the context and unfolding of such events reveal? Police chases, games of hide-and-seek with less hospitable neighbours, who might even 'turn informer', militant conversions (of a religious or political nature) in support of foreign families threatened with expulsion, burgeoning manifestations of solidarity in which emotions, indignation, and political criticism are intertwined, French citizens appearing in court on charges of assisting illegal immigrants to remain in France, the mobilization of various forms of media. We have come a long way from the ritual, domestic, and ordered practices of hospitality that, within the anthropological tradition, play an essential role in the understanding of social exchanges, and indeed in that of the transmission of social reproduction in general. The contemporary gestures of hospitality are explicitly 'voluntarist' and are the expression of personal commitments, usually justified on the grounds of the failings of the state and the 'shame' or 'indignation' that such failings provoke.

Encounters of a new type

Many new types of encounter are emerging as a result of this movement, which cuts across all European societies, in a political context where the term 'hospitality' has become synonymous with solidarity. It has generated, for example, the return of private hospitality, in other words the practice of individuals opening up their own homes, usually with the backing of some kind of organization capable of providing social and legal guarantees for this welcome at an individual level. This practice emerges as an extension of more collective gestures of solidarity, such as the distribution of food or clothing, help with language learning, and so on, either on the streets or in the premises of the various local organisations. It is shaped first of all by the relationship of individuals with their nation-state and by the expectations they have as citizens. In today's version of hospitality, a tripartite relationship is therefore established – one between migrants, the state, and ourselves. But it goes on to take the form of a face-to-face interaction for which our social system, particularly where family structures are concerned, is not – or no longer – really prepared.

In these conditions, hospitality is a challenge requiring a significant individual and collective commitment. Inevitably, among the members of the different organizations involved and among those who provide and receive accommodation there is sometimes a danger of various forms of overload (burnout of people working for organizations, 'overinvestment' on the part of hosts, 'family fatigue' experienced by guests). In the light of the general comments on hospitality set out here, current practices are an indication of the efforts undertaken in order to compensate for the disappearance of the social frameworks within which hospitality had for so long been confined.[1]

In the first instance it may be observed that hosts rarely act in isolation. It is as though there is a need to fill the social void left by increasingly individualized lifestyles, a reduction in family size, sometimes cramped living spaces, and finally the absence of any 'community' immediately active in the surrounding environment that could furnish a social link between the person receiving a guest and the guests themselves. In fact it is the various associations, themselves often grouped into networks on a city-wide scale, for example, and activist associations – or even, to a lesser degree, internet platforms – that provide the missing link and at the same time set out the rationale and the guidelines for welcoming guests into the home. Various systems of guarantee or of support provided by the associations protect each of the partners in the future relationship. For the associations involved, one of the major challenges is to prevent hosts from becoming disillusioned or anxious about the relationship established with their guests, after an initial and sometimes fleeting burst of solidarity. The level of respect felt for the persons to be hosted, their mental state, their personal dynamism, and the very fact that they are indeed in need of help are important criteria for their acceptance. In France in particular, the need to reassure hosts has also tended to bar those who are in an irregular situation from successfully finding accommodation.

In the same spirit, and in order to 'codify' somewhat a practice that it is more a matter of inventing than of re-establishing, associations and networks supporting the exchange of hospitality recommend minimum and maximum periods, which, moreover, can vary considerably. Depending on the individual case, the duration of stay can vary from between four and six weeks (the association assuming total responsibility for each migrant over a period of nine months), to anything between one and six months, with a minimum stay of four days. The turnover is important, with the result that the system is inevitably demanding in terms of the number of people involved in each individual case. In order to ensure that the relationship functions smoothly, organizations and associations take on the role of mediator and supervisor. Some of them try to ensure a frequent turnover in order to avoid the problem of attachment on the part of hosts. It is a matter of channelling the sometimes suffocating generosity of some and of reminding others not to ask their guests too many questions.

In reality, levels of commitment among hosts fluctuate. These are transgressive values which can be embodied in the practices associated with hospitality, with the risk that this might entail breaking the law, or something close to that. They depend on the season (for example, more offers of accommodation coincide with the implementation of a Plan grand froid (Cold Weather Plan), a national strategy implemented in extremely cold weather), on the availability of space for a guest in the family home and on the emotional impact of the initial experience. Lassitude and waning enthusiasm can leave organizations with an insufficient number of hosts to meet demand, or can result in their offer being simply scaled down according to availability. Furthermore, since these forms of hospitality effectively function in order to compensate, replace, or supplement public accommodation structures, they can end up being perceived as a sort of non-professionalized competition. This alarms public institutions, despite the fact that such institutions are clearly inadequate, particularly at a municipal level, as is the case in Paris.

Over a certain period of time and as a relationship is established between the host and his or her guest, administrative questions become more and more pressing. In some cases, people even begin to suspect that the person they are sheltering may not really have sufficient grounds to claim asylum. But, very often, the reasons justifying the migrant's presence in France and the question of his or her legitimacy, and indeed legality, gradually disappear as the relationship itself strengthens. An emotional relationship with the guest develops, particularly when he or she is considered to be a minor, in which case the host seeks to protect and educate the guest, no longer worrying about status.

There are also challenges to be faced by the guests, sometimes themselves taken aback by the 'intrusion' they are being invited to make into the lives of their hosts and hostesses and by the level of personal commitment that these are prepared to make on their behalf. If the arrangement does indeed free them from insecurity, life on the street or in temporary camps, they nevertheless remain wary and sometimes tire of being constantly urged to tell their stories. There are also occasions when they might suffer from 'family fatigue', as a result, for example, of the constant change of hosts and the attendant need to re-establish relationships, introduce themselves all over again, and so on.[2]

In one of these local associations, a 'mentor' from the organization is responsible for the welfare of those offered accommodation as they move from family to family. In other contexts, for instance in small towns or villages, the individual supervision of the migrant, whether minor or adult, over and above the issue of accommodation sometimes takes the form of a sponsorship whereby a member of the local population is nominated as a kind of godparent or sponsor to a migrant, under the supervision of a member of the municipal council. A system of legal, social, and moral support is therefore made available to anyone who has expressed a desire to welcome people into their homes by finding space for them or by offering them a room for their own use.

Some groups assert their willingness to practice 'civil disobedience' by supporting members of their association who take in migrants regardless of whether they have appropriate documents. This is the case of a Lille-based association called Migr'action, a network of individuals who organize themselves with a view to proposing temporary accommodation, at weekends, to migrants picked up in the Calais area (after the destruction of the temporary migrant camp in October 2016), providing them with a bed to sleep in, washing facilities and protection from aggressive police intervention. Members of the association take on the roles of drivers and hosts, picking up migrants in Calais, driving them to their homes in Lille for the weekend, and then taking them back again on Monday.

This Lille-based group draws inspiration from its Belgian neighbour, whose members take turns to provide shelter and transport for 500 migrants who are sleeping rough each weekend. In Brussels, migrants, the majority of whom come from Sudan and Eritrea, are looked after and offered accommodation by more than 30,000 volunteers (this was the figure in early 2018) who belong to the Citizen Platform in Support of Refugees created in 2014 via Facebook. These volunteers distribute food in Maximilian Park in the centre of the capital, then organize accommodation for migrants in private homes. As a result, every day hundreds of people are offered accommodation by private individuals. 'The government is constantly congratulating itself on the absence of a "jungle" in Brussels', says one of those involved, 'but it is thanks to us, thanks to the citizens who have taken it upon themselves to do the government's work rather than leave people out on the streets in the rain and the cold!'[3] On a number of occasions, the federal police have descended on the meeting place to arrest illegal immigrants and to challenge sympathetic members of the population. But this harassment produces the opposite effect to the one intended, drawing attention to and support for this movement: 'the Platform is expanding and its members are becoming more and more vociferous',[4] observes the European media network Euractiv.

An identical state of affairs and identical examples of civil disobedience can be found in Denmark, where The Friendly Neighbours, the Venligboerne movement set up in 2013, initially as a neighbourhood network, numbered in 2017 some 150,000 supporters, some of whom help migrants move around and find shelter. The movement's activities range from collecting food and clothing for refugees to opening a café where people bring in cakes and play music, setting up a car-sharing system designed to help refugees get from the Danish–German border to the Danish–Swedish border, and even into Sweden, and organising accommodation for migrants in people's homes. The last two activities are considered illegal and are subject to prosecution under human trafficking legislation.[5]

These brief notes on hospitality in contemporary contexts, limited as they are, are intended simply to put down a few markers. Thus, in Europe, with the surges of solidarity shown by individuals towards migrants and refugees in need of help, we can see various manifestations of the 'return' of hospitality. At the same time, we also become aware of its limitations in the form of a high turnover that is difficult to coordinate and relational contexts where the political, sociological, and intimate dimensions of hospitality overlap and even 'collide' in a single place and in a single interaction.

In addition to the problem of saturation, there is also an element of disproportion in that each supportive offer of accommodation represents a mere drop in the ocean of the global instability of the migration process, and the practice of private hospitality often turns out to be ambiguous, difficult, and challenging, both for hosts and for their guests. The limits in terms of space and social effectiveness in the private sphere are quickly reached, as are those on a local scale more generally. But if private hospitality has changed, it is primarily because the private world has also changed and because the gesture of hospitality has evolved from being a self-evident social activity, indistinguishable from general forms of sociality, to being a voluntarist and individual approach, defined by a sense of commitment and by an emotional, ethical, and political investment.

Hospitality: causes and effects

Collectives and associations such as those referred to above, whether long-standing or newly established, take on the role, and sometimes even the vocation, of providing a social framework and a meaning (religious, political, societal) to an individual practice of hospitality that has to a great extent been 'updated' in the context of twenty-first-century Europe. Their exceptional levels of engagement represent one of the most significant public causes in European societies today. This phenomenon has led certain citizens to express their commitment through and for hospitality, which has come to symbolize their disagreement with the way the state treats foreigners. The migrants' cause, which underlies that of hospitality, is not, however, uniform and can be better understood in the plural. It seemed to me possible in this case to identify four distinct causes, which I shall briefly summarize here.[6]

We can choose to help migrants in the name of human suffering. But compassion assumes that the other person, who is the intended object of our emotion, is afflicted, in other words diminished. Or even dead. The emotional outpouring provoked by the image of a dead child on a Turkish beach in September 2015 is a striking example of this humanitarian cause. But we should not forget the political context of that particular moment. Over the course of the preceding weeks, there had been unprecedented support for the opening up of borders, but the German chancellor only agreed to this measure just one week before the photograph of little Aylan was made public. Put another way, humanitarian emotion is not an absolute value but one that is rooted in a political context.

We can also choose to help migrants in the name of similarity, a motivation that is, literally (and not ideologically), 'identity'-based. Identification is indeed one of the more common triggers for concern. Very often, those seeking to demonstrate their support for migrants are heard to announce: 'I myself am the son or daughter of a migrant, a refugee,' and so on. The cause, in this case, amounts to taking care of the other because he or she represents the other me that I carry in myself ... at the somewhat narcissistic risk of being disappointed because this other, all too real, cannot necessarily be reduced to my own identity.

This solidarity can also manifest itself in the name of difference, or what might be termed the 'exotic' cause. It involves seeing migrants as the epitome of everything we are not, that 'other' we are in need of. The danger here lies in oversimplifying the differences and in seeing migrants only in terms of this difference, whereas in fact they are – or aspire to be – modern, connected, mobile. In reality these others are constantly changing, just as we are, and mobility reinforces the dynamic of the cultural changes each one experiences.

Finally, when we see heroes and adventurers among the migrants, commendation of their singularity, which represents a fourth cause, runs the risk of blinding us to the collective reasons – political, social, or climatic – that lie behind these examples of contemporary mobility: the state of the world, in fact. Migrants themselves are at pains to point this out whenever we have dealings with them, drawing attention to the political responsibilities behind their situation, responsibilities that lie in their countries of origin or in those they pass through, as well as in their host countries. There are exiled political voices that are barely heard today, yet nevertheless continue to speak out.

My intention is, clearly, not to judge, and still less to validate or invalidate the different causes behind a commitment to the dignified treatment of migrants, and even the decision to welcome them into the home. It is simply to say that none of them is pure and perfect, absolute, sacred, or unquestionable and that we should continue to look beyond them. The critical gaze that is turned on these 'causes' confines itself to putting them into perspective, allowing them to be questioned and challenged. Such a gaze is not aimed at people, since nobody is restricted to any one of these causes or permanently trapped in the position indicated by his or her first instinct. This is precisely because, in the diversity of their *raisons d'être*, of their motives, and of the feelings, beliefs, or convictions that influence the 'hosts', the 'friendly neighbours', or the 'committed citizens' in different ways, these experiences transform individuals in their relationships both with the nation-state and with strangers – two concepts that are significant factors in understanding today's world.

If these causes therefore have specific effects on those who espouse them, they also have an impact on the people who find themselves on the receiving end of their hospitality.

In order to deal with this question, I would like to refer to an encounter that took place on 5 March 2018 at the University of Paris 8. At that time a number of migrants, asylum seekers, or undocumented individuals with nowhere to stay had occupied part of the university buildings for several weeks, with the logistical and political support of students and of some members of the teaching staff, which meant they could stay put and, to a certain extent, begin to feel established on the premises. On that particular occasion, two faculty members had organized an evening of discussion and solidarity: 'In support of asylum. An alternative immigration policy is possible.'[7] In the packed lecture theatre there were many students, teachers from the university and from elsewhere, as well as those occupying part of the buildings.

From 6.30 p.m. onwards, various support associations were given the opportunity to speak, followed by teachers and researchers, and then, around 9.30 p.m., some of the new occupants of the premises indicated that they wanted an opportunity to speak. The first to do so was an Ethiopian asylum seeker whose case had already been dismissed several times. He was clearly a seasoned political militant who had serious problems in his own country. He began his speech with these words, which I wrote down in exact detail: 'We would like to thank you. You have treated us like your own children by offering us shelter within your university, but we are not yet satisfied.' What followed touched on the situation in Ethiopia, the collusion between European and African governments, and so on. But the first words of his speech contained almost all the terms of the debate and of the 'conflict of opinion' inherent in hospitality that I have sought to draw attention to: 'We would like to thank you' – because we must say thank you, it is one of the codes of hospitality. 'You have treated us like your own children' – because hospitality represents an asymmetric relationship in which the guest is the *yaro*, the 'child', just as we saw earlier among the Hausas in West Africa, where the person offering hospitality says to his or her guest: 'You are my child [*yaro*], you do as you wish, I look after you in my own home'; but clearly 'you are my child' – or, reciprocally, 'you have treated me like your child' – indicates a relationship based on dependence. 'You have treated us like your own children by offering us somewhere to stay', in other words by providing shelter, that little bit of space that enables us to have the minimum needed to live; and hospitality is therefore brought back down to this, to the necessary minimum, by the person receiving it. As we have seen, the ritual of hospitality in the strict sense of the term, a ritual revealed here in its true light by the speaker's intervention, can, depending on the era and the place, last for three, ten or twelve days, and the space allocated is equally clearly defined, for example a room near the entrance of the house. 'But we are not yet satisfied': what the orator is saying here is that there is something else that needs to be talked about, a request of an entirely different nature.

Should we give up using the word 'hospitality' altogether and replace it with the adage wheeled out on every possible occasion by the mayor of Grande-Synthe: 'No-one should die of hunger and cold within my municipality'? Or should we call this a 'principle of hospitality', hold on to it, and ask ourselves what it would take for it to become a superior principle, which would have the force of law and would not therefore depend at all, or at least not exclusively, on the goodwill of individuals? To avoid confining ourselves simply to the notion of a favour, or to a slogan, we need to broaden the question, further extend the 'surface' of our inquiry into what hospitality means in the different worlds in which we, hosts and strangers, live. That would enable us to investigate other scales of action, which are the potential contexts for common action – most realistically local, perhaps even national, and global in a manner possibly less utopian than might be suggested.

An adequate response to the phenomenon of migration movements in the world today, to their enduring presence and expanding scale, will require considerably more than private hospitality. Close inspection of real situations indicates that an intermediary form of intervention is emerging in a relatively new way, even if here too there is no lack of historical precedents. This form of intervention lies somewhere between the individualized context of the domestic sphere and the anonymity of the nation-state and represents a different manifestation of hospitality, which is that associated with towns and villages. A closer inspection is called for.

The emergence of municipal hospitality

A key question that arises, as we have seen so far, in a largely systematic way concerns the *existing mechanisms* within which today's practice of hospitality is being integrated. If these mechanisms provide a framework for individual expressions of commitment, they also lead to a potential change of scale in both the practice and the conception of hospitality. Associations, local organizations, delocalized internet platforms, and national networks of associations are examples of some of these mechanisms. In 2017 a network of associations published a map of France that represented 'one thousand citizen-led initiatives for solidarity with migrants', including 200 local organizations or associations dedicated to providing them with accommodation.[8] Similarly, a network of *élus hospitaliers*, 'elected representatives welcoming migrants', has existed in northern France since 2012. This network led to the establishment, in 2018, of a 'national association of welcoming towns' (which includes Briançon, the first arrondissement in Lyons, Ivry, Grenoble, Villeurbanne, Grande-Synthe, Montreuil, etc.).

In Italy, the 'integrated reception' strategy of the Protection System for Asylum and Refugee Seekers

(SPRAR) favours local networks of hospitality. Large villages and small towns are mobilized to welcome migrants and, as a result, are themselves transformed, like the now famous example of the village of Riace in Calabria. A victim of emigration for many years and with many of its houses abandoned, the village experienced a spectacular transformation with the arrival of Kurdish immigrants in 1998, which was followed by other, similar waves during the years 2000 and 2010. The deeply committed, charismatic, and high-profile mayor of the village, with the backing of the national protection system for refugees and asylum seekers (SPRAR) and some European Union funding, is the man behind this story of a 'virtuous circle' of hospitality.[9] This is also underpinned by the emphatic revival of a 'local culture of hospitality', as exemplified by the ritual of the *visita* practised between the houses of the village and symbolically reconfigured as the basis for the Riace model. Not only has the village become a model of integration, but it has been repopulated (in 2017 it had around 2,000 inhabitants, including 600 refugees and asylum seekers). Baïgorri in the Basque Country,[10] Barcelonnette, or Trébeurden in Brittany, with its 'Comité des gens heureux d'accueillir des migrants' ('Committee of People Happy to Welcome Migrants') set up in 2017, all offer similar versions of village-based hospitality.

Faced with the unexpected arrival of migrants – in small groups or in their hundreds or thousands, as the case may be – certain towns have begun to explore the idea of a policy designed to welcome and accommodate migrants, one capable of adapting to international mobility, given that this situation will be ongoing. Concepts such as 'welcoming towns', 'migrant houses', or 'welcoming neighbourhoods' have therefore begun to emerge in the domains of architecture, urbanization, and redevelopment, alongside discussions on the use of squats and industrial wastelands, gradually setting in place a range of technical options and sparking off just as many political debates. For, beyond the solutions envisaged and implemented to varying extents, according to the capacity of the towns and countries concerned, two fundamental questions need to be addressed. On the one hand, there is the nature of the links that the municipal authorities have established with the local population and the migrants and, on the other, the towns' desire and capacity for autonomy vis-à-vis the central, national government. In short, a reinvention of municipal hospitality is emerging in many urban initiatives, seminars, planning or municipal council meetings, and in the course of local or national public debates that have taken place over the past few years on the subject of the welcome, settlement, and movement of migrants in towns and cities.[11]

What form does this municipal hospitality take? If we compare the situations of French towns such as Calais, Grande-Synthe, or Paris, for example, over the past few years, it is clear that several forms of welcome (or non-welcome) exist. In purely practical terms, space needs to be found somewhere within the boundaries of the municipality, or a commitment to find such a space needs to be agreed, and this is often achieved with a certain amount of improvisation on the part of councillors or of their municipal officers, and as a matter of urgency. Shanty towns and squats raise questions around the 'ghettoization' of migrants, and I shall return to this urban phenomenon. And migrant houses appear on a regular basis and are often seen as the most desirable option by social workers and associations.

From ghetto to migrant houses

If the shanty town represents the most obvious urban form it is not the result of any moral conviction or from the point of view of democratic values, but simply as a reflection of what is actually going on in the world. For the sake of understanding as well as of action, it is interesting to look more closely at this urban phenomenon of the shanty town and, beyond it, of the ghetto, a term frequently associated with it. For most people, these words suggest an extremely negative image. If we suspend all judgement and go back in time, we see for example that the first ghetto in history, in sixteenth-century Venice, took shape as a result of a 'decree of segregation'. That decree, promulgated by the city council of Venice on 29 March 1516, compelled the city's Jews to confine themselves between nightfall and dawn to a block of buildings situated on a small island, previously the site of a foundry (*ghetto*, which therefore gave its name to the Jewish quarter) and where the Jewish Museum of Venice is now located. It was only in 1797 that a new town council inspired by the French Revolution, and a 'Committee for public health', abolished this loathsome segregation, removed the gates from the ghetto and accorded Jews the same civil rights as any other citizens of Venice. But it is worth noting that, after the first decree of segregation at the beginning of the sixteenth century, the ghetto became the enforced meeting place for any wandering Jews, seafarers, and traders subsequently arriving in Venice as foreigners, without there being any significant common ground in terms of language, history, or religious rituals between the established Jewish population and the newcomers. Originating from Germany, France, Italy, the Middle East, and Spain, they did not form any kind of homogenous social or cultural whole.[12]

Today we find almost these exact words reproduced in certain phrases uttered in the context of the arrival of migrants in a city: 'You can go there, you are allowed to go there, you will be tolerated there.' In a sense, it is this same 'decree' that the prefecture of Pas-de-Calais adopted towards the Calais migrants in April 2015 when it granted them authorization to occupy a single area – notably the 'wasteland' near the Jules-Ferry Day Centre, where they would be 'tolerated'. An almost word for word rendering of the segregation decree associated with the very first ghetto.

People who make up the population of shanty towns must have somehow found themselves grouped together in order to arrive in a certain place and decide to settle there, and it is by no means inevitable that this community will necessarily be the product of one single ethnic or racial identity. Individuals simply came together as a community at a given moment, arriving and settling in that particular place, in a context where the town as a whole, and as a desirable focal point, was forbidden to them either in fact or in law. It is a process we see re-enacted all over the world, taking the form of a sequence of events beginning with the moment of arrival or 'invasion' (as the favelas in certain Latin American cities are known), the taking over and settling of a given space followed by the adaptation and improvement of that space, and eventually even permanent settlement.

In both the shanty town and the ghetto, even bearing in mind the many geographical and historical disparities between them, it is clearly the town or the city that, through its relationship with foreigners and strangers, creates its own fringes. The pejorative connation of the ghetto comes later, greatly complicating matters and rendering any form of understanding much more difficult because, in the meanwhile, the social world, segregated within the ghetto, has nevertheless existed in a state of marginalization and in relative separation. The strangers (outsiders, those who come from outside) settled there because they had no other choice, then they began to have families, the seeds of a shared culture were sown, political relationships began to take shape ... At that stage, the ghetto could be described as the urban social form that develops in a context of confinement. Without making any value judgements, it will simply be observed that, in a way that will be viewed positively by some and negatively by others, everything grows, transforms, or develops. Cultural products that end up being universally embraced are born in ghettos – like jazz for example, originating in the black American ghetto and associated with suffering and with the pain of segregation. Forms of political expression also develop, and these can take the form of opposition, of revolt, or even of mutual agreement, of conciliation with the neighbouring town or city. Furthermore, the word 'ghetto' exists on a global scale and has come to be seen as a rallying cry, a recognition of all forms of resistance of a cultural or ethnic nature that somehow reach beyond the limits of their place of origin and refer to some marginal condition in relation to a dominant order.

For example, in the Palestinian camps, political culture clung on to a certain idea about the camp for a considerable time: people were living there in the expectation of a return to the land of Palestine, which meant that they kept the key of their lost homes, and there was a prevailing culture based on the notion of a return. Nowadays, for the young Palestinian militants, the demand for any kind of return is much less prevalent than that of being allowed to live where they are, to transform the area of the camp, to urbanize it, and to build on it. They are working with architects, urban planners, and designers. And the place itself is more and more often referred to as a 'ghetto' and no longer as a 'camp'. Young Palestinian rappers say 'We are living in a ghetto' rather than 'We are living in a camp.' In order to be listened to in and beyond the place assigned to them, they are turning to the 'universal face of the ghetto'.[13] There is a generational split between the older people, who refer to the camp as a place of exile and continue to support the political claim for a great return, and the younger generation who talk about the ghetto in the sense of an urban reality. By using the word 'ghetto' they lay claim to an urban status of their own. More generally, this word is now used on a global scale to describe the culture of those who suffer from oppression, the black culture that is becoming increasingly globalized. And at that level, identification in terms of space becomes less necessary and significant.

In American history, the Chicago ghetto, for example, was originally, between 1920 and 1930, a Jewish ghetto, but gradually the Jews began to leave the ghetto and move into the city itself. From that point onwards, the ghetto became the area where black migrants from the south of the United States would arrive. The ghetto therefore took on a role that Louis Wirth, a Chicago urban sociologist, wrote about in the mid-1920s, when he described the ghetto as 'a transitional stage'.[14] This is more generally true in relation to the urban status of areas attributed to foreigners. Thus, in West Africa, the *Zongo* districts, originally occupied by an ethnic group – the Hausas – became, in the course of their history (from the mid-nineteenth-century onwards), the 'strangers' quarters', as they are somewhat generically called. And these, too, served as a kind of transitional zone. They were, in a literal sense, the 'reception zones' from where the families of migrants or their descendants gradually gained entry into the city – a process that could be spread over the course of two or three generations.

The ghetto is a form of urban space with a history of its own. This history enables us to interrogate the present, for example, by asking ourselves whether a particular place is currently the result of a decree of segregation. It is this separation, or 'apartheid', as it is beginning to be referred to in France, that creates the

ghetto: the city promulgates a decree of segregation on
the grounds that certain groups need to be kept separate
and confined to the margins of other areas, thus
confirming the status of these areas as central zones.
The principle used to group people under the decree of
segregation of April 2015, which resulted in the Calais
shanty town camp, was not based on cultural identity
or on some specific ethnicity, but on a relationship to
the other, the stranger, the migrant. A policy of hostility,
it might be said, mirroring the debate on the policy of
hospitality with which we are more broadly concerned
here, resulted in the authorities' decision to set aside
this isolated area for a group of people who found
themselves classed as outsiders. However, as that space
has now been destroyed, no further development took
place and the area did not become either a ghetto or
the town that was already beginning to take shape.[15]
For, as a public policy, tolerance is constantly in danger
of running out. Tolerance is not a right but, at best, a
favour granted with respect to a particular space and
for a limited period of time. In this sense it can, in
certain circumstances, be compatible with the practices
associated with hospitality.

In Africa, the occupation of buildings abandoned as
a result of war sometimes continues over the course of
many years, in the form of self-administrated squats on
a very large scale. On the outer edges of Monravia, the
capital of Liberia, this was the destiny of the Voice of
America (VoA) building – an American radio station
well known in Africa. A long building, three stories
high, it had been abandoned by the Americans because
of the war. Only the basic concrete structure was left
standing. Those who had taken up residence there had
organized the space into a number of different areas
that were crudely delineated. There were more or less
isolated areas for cooking, and blankets were used to
separate private spaces. With no water, no electricity,

and no sanitation system, comfort was minimal. Among the residents there were internally displaced Liberians who had not yet decided whether to return home to the north of the country, as well as Sierra-Leonean refugees who were not far from their county's border but were reluctant to go back, since they felt that Sierra Leone was not stable enough for them to contemplate a return.

The model of a tower transformed into a squat can be found in many different cities. Take, for example, the case of the Gaza Hospital, a squat established in the Sabra district of Beirut in 1987 by Palestinians (both men and women) fleeing the 'internal war' in the Chatila camp a few hundred metres away. The building had been completely deserted a few months earlier, after a fire that damaged several floors. The Syrian army, which was at that point occupying the Sabra zone, gave the fleeing Palestinians permission to take up residence in the semi-ruined building. 'Then, in the space of three days, people started turning up, and it was full', explains one of the three women who originally founded the site. Controlled today by two Palestinian families who invested considerably in the transformation of the building, the Gaza Hospital squat houses Palestinian and Lebanese Palestinian families, Syrian families who have been settled there for some time, and, more recently, migrant workers and many Syrian refugees, but also Egyptian and Sudanese migrants – and, finally, migrants from Bangladesh, the most recent arrivals. The latter rent basement rooms that were built by the son of one of the two main families associated with the squat.

There are now in total some 127 apartments of varying sizes (one or two rooms for the most part and, much more rarely, three or four rooms) and about 500 inhabitants. From eight floors when it first opened, the squat now extends over ten floors, and an eleventh one is currently under construction. No-one has any title documents, yet it is clear without significant conflict which residents are owners, which are housed for free and which are tenants. For a small number of people, the squat has become a source of investment (construction work) and of profit (rents), even though the overall impression is that of a 'vertical favela' with only rudimentary arrangements regarding sanitation, the supply of water and electricity, and refuse collection or drainage. Norwegian Refugee Council (NRC), a Norwegian NGO, intervened in 2008, with support from the European Community Humanitarian Aid Office (ECHO), to improve sanitary conditions in the building.

In many ways, the Gaza Hospital could be regarded as an extension of the Chatila camp. In everyday life, the few hundred meters separating the two locations are quickly covered, and family and friendship bonds remain strong. But its history is not just Palestinian; it also reflects the history of conflicts in the Middle East and a very 'global' economic pattern, with the movement of workers – Syrian, Egyptian, North and South Sudanese, Sri-Lankan, Bangladeshi, and Ethiopian migrants – for whom the squat represents one possible way of accessing the city. And it is, after all, an urban story, that of the city of Beirut, that makes Sabra a separate moral region, very different today from the 'Palestinian zone' it was between 1960 and 1970. Sabra is described by Beirut media sources as a 'cosmopolitan poverty zone', and the Gaza Hospital squat is a perfect embodiment of this. Even though relatively settled (the oldest residents have lived there for between twenty and thirty years), the people who inhabit the Gaza Hospital always see themselves as being in a state of transit. The Palestinian and Syrian refugees are waiting (or claim to be waiting) to return to the land they were driven out of, and the migrants see their transit through the Gaza Hospital as simply one stage in a longer cycle of mobility.[16]

The general trend, as witnessed in numerous countries throughout the world, is to allow the most deprived migrants to move in near those city dwellers who are the poorest and most marginalized in terms of urban integration and, more generally, in terms of a right to the city. This convergence of vulnerable groups is probably not exactly what the utopian notion of a 'welcoming city' might aspire to, but it is nevertheless a process that can be observed in Europe in those countries where public intervention in the reception of migrants is minimal. Migrant squats are therefore officially tolerated right next to social housing, at the risk of reinforcing a sense of exclusion both in the more recent migrants and in those from the poorer neigh-bourhoods where they have been allowed to settle.

This is exactly what happened in the area around the Place des Fêtes in the 19th arrondissement in Paris, where the abandoned premises of the former Lycée Jean-Quarré were occupied from 31 July to 23 October 2015.[17] The inhabitants of this working-class and disadvantaged area, who are often themselves from immigrant families or descended from immigrants and refugees, have been fighting for many years to obtain more help from the city council to improve living conditions in the area and to set in place social and cultural initiatives. They were abruptly confronted by the sudden arrival of the migrants and their militant supporters who had been driven out of the camps at Porte de la Chapelle at the end of July 2015. Less than three days after their arrival, the city council announced its agreement to 'tolerate' the occupation officially, then went on to outline plans to transform the former secondary school into a centre for urgent temporary accommodation rather than into the multimedia library that local people had been campaigning for over the course of many years and to which the council had already signalled its commitment. This distant generosity towards the migrants left the impression 'of a sort of abandonment in this neighbourhood of north-east Paris and of contempt for its inhabitants'.[18] By way of a policy to welcome the migrants, the City of Paris left the local people without any support to face the considerable task of coming to the aid of the new arrivals and of managing relations with the hundreds of migrants present (150 on day one, the number had risen to 1,404 on the day when the site was evacuated). This policy generated a certain amount of hostility among some residents who resented being forced to accept the presence of these new neighbours, but also generated a compensatory solidarity among some others who were critical of an abandonment on the part of public authorities, of which they already saw themselves as victims.

In the three-part relationship I have referred to here – between migrants, our state, and 'ourselves' – where the local inhabitants' commitment regarding hospitality is determined, it was the intermediary public authority that proved to be at fault in the first instance. The City of Paris had, in a sense, imposed a 'duty of hospitality' on local residents without providing any of the material, economic, or human resources required. Nevertheless, a substantial network of solidarity quickly established itself. A collective was set up – the group Solidarité Migrants Place des Fêtes (Solidarity with Migrants in the Place des Fêtes) – and another group, already in existence – Les Mères en place (Mothers at the Ready) – a collective of 30 or so local African women – was reinvigorated. French lessons, cooked meals, health care, support with administrative matters were all made available and social events, evening activities, and celebrations were organised ... The social mobilis-ation involved made the migrants' stay in the area safer and less stressful and also reinforced relationships between the local residents themselves, strengthening their interactions and their attachment to the area. But, in the end, if the experience was in many ways a remarkable one, it nevertheless left a bitter aftertaste. 'Some time afterwards', Isabelle Coutant observes, 'I learned that the Château Landon barracks, where an initial occupation by migrants had been turned down by the City authorities in June 2015 – just before the occupation of Jean-Quarré – was going to be transformed into an "incubator for fashion businesses," in keeping with the surrounding gentrification of the area. A clear case of a different neighbourhood, different issues, different priorities?'[19] The accommodation centre was indeed scheduled to open at the beginning of 2016, on the site previously occupied, and would be run by the charity Emmaüs[20] and financed by the state and any plans for the multi-media library in the same location have been shelved. Furthermore, unlike the 'Centre for Refugees' (as its supporters called it), the centre for urgent temporary accommodation is no longer open to all. Any contacts between local residents and migrants have gradually dwindled.

In keeping with the integrated reception strategy observed in numerous villages in Italy and in many small towns throughout the whole of Europe, the model of the 'migrant house' (offering accommodation and other support under one roof) presents an alternative to the practice of separation and distancing that result in the urban forms of the shanty town, the ghetto, or squats in industrial premises, in public buildings, or in abandoned apartment blocks such as the ones described here. Migrant houses exist in numerous places around the world, especially near borders. For example, at Tijuana, in the north of Mexico, on the border with the United States, a local priest, who is seen in the town as a pillar of hospitality, has taken charge of a building in the town. Run by a militant Catholic association, La Casa de Migrantes is an old building that has seen various other uses in the past and is constructed around an open patio area. Migrants know that they can come and sleep there, sometimes for an extended period, and encounter other migrants, of their own nationality or from other countries.

In the Sahel region of Africa, too, the term 'migrant house' is used to refer to empty houses where migrants are allowed to squat. These become well-known landmarks on migratory routes, which are increasingly used in Niger, Chad, or Mali. Very much part of the urban fabric, these houses are transformed into places designated for use by migrants, with strong links to the associations that offer them support and, in particular, provide them with food.

Calais and its surrounding area remain a special case, with a large influx of migrants that shows no signs of diminishing, no matter what kind of reception they can expect to find. The border is difficult to cross and creates a permanent bottleneck. In this context, instead of the camps, squats, and 'jungles' that have been in place for more than fifteen years, the concept of *maisons des migrants* ('migrant houses') was proposed by a group of associations known as PSM (La Plateforme de service aux migrants / Service Platform for Migrants) in 2013, with the backing of the network of *élus hospitaliers*, (elected representatives welcoming migrants). The project favours structures of a modest size, envisaged as 'places of temporary shelter for migrants in transit', with the capacity to accommodate between twenty and thirty people. Managed thanks to a collaboration between professionals, militant groups and migrants, the proposed *maisons des migrants* would be seen as private from a legal perspective. Regarded as experimental by the network of associations behind the project, the plan has not yet received any state support, nor has it been taken up at a municipal level.

Hospitable municipality versus hostile state

Everywhere, and particularly in France, commentary and actions at a municipal level in support of a (re) invention of forms of public hospitality inevitably raise the question of the relationship between town and state. It is a case of envisaging (and perhaps of imagining) what it is that towns and cities are capable of doing, which the state cannot or will not do. This was the starting point of the EU Charter of Cities of Asylum adopted on the initiative of the International Parliament of Writers, whose aims were outlined by Derrida in the following terms: 'If we refer to the city, rather than to the State, it is because we have expectations of a new concept of the city, which we have almost abandoned hope of achieving from the State.' Derrida continues:

> the concept in which we have placed our hopes and called the 'city of asylum' is no longer merely a device consisting of new attributes or new powers added on to the classic, unaltered concept of the City. We are no longer dealing with new predicates to enrich the old subject called 'City'. No, we are dreaming of another concept, another right, another policy for the City.[21]

It is without illusion (and echoing his appeal for an 'unconditional hospitality', outlined in the same speech and then returned to in other texts, discussed earlier) that Derrida refers to the disparity between a local sovereignty, which goes back to the era of medieval 'free towns', and another reality, represented by the current state of political, sovereign, national, and international configurations. Without illusion, because the two realities do not carry the same weight in the empirical actualization of the utopia in which he is interested, that of the cities of asylum. But, in doing so, he articulates a political strategy that enables

the current choices, which might otherwise appear
to be self-evident (protecting a territory, considering
the foreigner as an enemy, etc.) to be put to the test.
These choices are locked in an argument for which
the moral and political logic has been laid down in
advance, as a truth that cannot be undone from within
(like Foucault's 'order of discourse'). The language of
the cities of asylum, which goes back to a historical
principle – the medieval principle that *quid est in territorio est de territorio* ('whatever is in the territory is
of the territory'): 'those who are here are from here',
declares Derrida, with reference to Hannah Arendt –
shifts the debate, allowing for the possibility of political
dissent (*dissensus*). The possibility that the city should
be elevated above the nation-state, or should at least
break free from it, is the question, the programme
even, proposed by the model of the cities of asylum
championed by Derrida, which is now actually being
put into effect by certain towns and cities.

With 'sanctuary cities' (to borrow a term used by
various American municipalities seeking to demonstrate
their willingness to offer shelter to illegal immigrants
and refusing to denounce them to the authorities),
'asylum cities' (*Venezia città dell'asilo*), even 'solidarity
cities' (the Solidarity Cities movement of the European
left), and indeed 'rebel cities' (Barcelona with its Mayor
Ada Colau, former leader of movements protecting the
rights of squatters in the city), the utopia of asylum
cities is becoming an attainable horizon, albeit still a
distant one, given the uneven degree of determination to
achieve it. Although still very much in the minority, this
experience 'is evidence of an alternative approach, often
one that goes against national policies'.[22] And, according
to Filippo Furri, the current redeployment of political
municipal sovereignty in relation to this issue echoes
more widely 'neo-municipalist tendencies in Europe,
calling for increased autonomy for municipalities on

social issues, but also on environmental, economic, and political ones'.[23]

This is a form of political logic that we see emerging in a number of countries and that disturbs the natural order of institutions. To what degree can a city or a village free itself from the yoke of the state, challenge its authority, and openly disagree with it? The Parisian experience is an interesting one in this respect. In 2016 Anne Hidalgo, the mayor of Paris, signed a European appeal for refugee cities initiated by her counterpart in Barcelona, Ada Colau, and joined forces with other mayors of major cities to publicly defend the need to welcome exiles in general. Yet the humanitarian camp set up at Porte de la Chapelle in Paris in the spring of 2016, after that established at Grande-Synthe a few months earlier (with its accompanying national media success), was immediately taken over and managed by the prefecture. As a result, it became a zone of transition – not to the city itself, but to the various processes involved in requests for asylum in the Paris region – with the attendant spiral of queues, makeshift camps, and violent dispersals by the police. And in this instance the resumption of control by the prefecture, and therefore by the state, was not challenged by the municipal authorities.

The size of cities is of course an important parameter, and the status of capital city gives Paris a significant demographic and political weight in France. Consequently, it is no surprise that the mayor of Paris should immediately find herself on the national political stage. Logically, she could therefore adopt a supranational discourse, like that of the major cities (London, New York, Madrid, Barcelona, Palermo), in whose wake she apparently follows and which have opted for the kind of 'neo-municipalist' direction described here, thanks to the capacity for autonomy from their national governments that their economic and political power enables them to exercise. However, until now, the mayor of Paris has placed herself at the level of the French nation-state and in consequence finds herself locked in a position where, so firmly anchored is she in national politics, she cannot even take the kind of action she claims to support in favour of hospitality. What form might be taken by a political discourse corresponding to the level of the world city and asylum city she would like Paris to embody? It would certainly bring her closer to two other real and effective anchorage points: the local and the global.

In Germany, in Italy, or in Spain, the states, the regions, and the provinces as well as the European Community support a certain number of municipal initiatives or local networks of associations. In such cases, a relationship is established on a local level and with the various associations, as though to represent the beginning of an accommodation policy that adopts a principle of hospitality as a prerequisite. But, even if we assume that one day these solutions will indeed exist alongside each other, for now they are no more than the first indications of the history of a mobile world.

3

The Need for Cosmopolitics

So let us rethink hospitality. Let us take it a step or two further. Preferably two steps. Because, as René Schérer suggests,[1] at the national level hospitality is a 'catastrophe', given the fundamental incompatibility between its territorial restrictions and freedom of movement. Even if the mayor of Paris, the mayor of Sevran (a community in the Parisian suburbs with residents from almost eighty different nationalities), or the mayor of London willingly proclaim that they represent world cities, we have yet to hear a head of state refer to his or her country as a 'world nation'. Emmanuel Kant himself, although the strongest advocate of 'universal hospitality', fell into this trap, by making the nation-state the basic unit of international order, even though its attendant restrictions ended up distorting his principle of hospitality. Nor can there be 'state hospitality', or any 'national policy of hospitality', for that would be equivalent to erecting a 'national house' and restricting access according to the will of the proprietor – an 'I invite into my home whomever I want' transposed from the individual home to the nation.

Cosmopolitanism today

The intellectual approach taken by the Enlightenment philosopher is nevertheless of interest to us because, although it ultimately locks itself within the limits of the 'stato-national' model, it sets out to be a theory of the individual within the wider world. In this sense, it is indeed a liberal individualist utopia.[2] It is precisely this conflict – between individuals and their individual characteristics on the one hand, nations and state structures on the other – in the face of the need for cosmopolitics, that today allows this to become an argument in the context of contemporary debates, as an active principle, albeit one that is contradictory – and thus, to a certain extent, incomplete. Alongside states and individuals as 'citizens of the world', Kant also had in mind the utopian concept of a world society. For this reason, although the writing of those two forward-looking essays, *Idea for a Universal History with a Cosmopolitan Intent* and *To Perpetual Peace: A Philosophical Sketch*, dates back more than two centuries, his words and his ideas are still strikingly pertinent. We rediscovered these ideas with the ending of the East–West conflict, the opening up of markets to globalisation, and the technical capacity to travel anywhere on the planet at ever increasing speeds, and even to be instantly transported elsewhere thanks to the internet. There is a growing sense that we can all share the same world – a world whose final common frontier is currently the natural limit of the planet we call Earth. From this point on, we should have no further hesitation in considering ourselves 'earthlings' or 'terrestrials'.[3] The discovery of the earth's ecological oneness, of our interdependence and of our collective responsibility in this context, can once again, and in a different manner from that of the age of Enlightenment, give our era the task of transposing this ecological oneness into a political oneness, rendered conceivable by the ending of the Cold War. Conceptions that are, in varying degrees, enthusiastic, utopian, joyous, or anxious have emerged as a result of this notion of the planet as a single entity. Nor is there any shortage of arguments. Our planet is a finite whole that each person can embrace and even 'see' in its totality, a totality from which no one and nowhere is excluded. It is a round surface, and one from which there is therefore no escape from others. And, finally, it is a potentially shared world, one in which thought and politics can be envisaged on a world scale and can be literally 'realistic', since they have found their reality: the planet itself. So what has become of this cosmo-political notion today?

In the course of her research on urban cosmo-politanisms, the sociologist Louise Carlier focused her attention on two major authors from the early twentieth century who have inspired sociological studies on this subject: the German writer Georg Simmel and the American author Robert Ezra Park. She observes that their approaches to cosmopolitanism were developed as a response to the evils of their time: German nationalism in the case of Simmel, who focused in particular on the figure of the stranger, free to come and go at will; and racial and urban segregation in the case of Park, a close observer of the city of Chicago, with a particular interest in the social and moral disorganisation of this mosaic of a city.[4] Kant's cosmopolitanism could similarly be placed in the context of a reflective and critical re-examination on the part of the eighteenth-century Enlightenment of the colonial conquests that had gone before it, as a delayed response to the 'encounter' between Europeans and Indian, American, and African peoples, to the domination, violence and massacres that were played out in these regions, and to attempts at reciprocal understanding. This response, between two and three centuries later, could only be the quest for 'perpetual peace' within a humanity at once unified from one end of the planet to the other and diverse, capable of avoiding war by allowing the triumph of reason, and thus enabling humankind to escape from 'this chaotic state of national relations' and to find a balanced 'cosmopolitan state'.[5]

And for us, today, what contemporary evil are we trying to address by re-examining the question of cosmopolitanism? The mobility that we cherish for ourselves, the freedom to go wherever we choose, is in the throes of becoming a global tragedy for millions of ordinary people just like you and me, and fatal for tens of thousands of others. The Mediterranean, the Mexican Desert, the Sahara, the Bay of Bengal have turned into graveyards of the universal. A global anthropological imbalance renders part of humanity worthless, instantly forgettable and sacrificed at the very moment when mobility is generally perceived as highly desirable or as an indispensable means of escape from crises – simply in order to be able to work, live, and participate in the world in the broadest possible sense. Yet this 'other' section of humanity, which risks death by becoming part of the flow of international migration, is not a single and homogeneous entity in time, space, and culture. It does not have a specific identity, it is unstable, changing, a radical (or 'radicalised') embodiment of the stranger who can be encountered anywhere on the planet. This is what we need to overcome and to find a solution for, regardless of the 'cause' that has led us to this point. Fear itself, and an obsession with security, can just as easily be a motivating force, a reason to rethink hospitality and cosmopolitanism and to be suspicious of the words emanating from the leaders of nation-states. For what could be more dangerous than cultivating the reassuring image of a cossetted, protected, and desirable world of luxury, glitter, and justice while at the same time selecting those entitled to enter and keeping at bay a growing mass of the supernumerary?[6]

The principle of hospitality and cosmopolitics from a philosophical perspective

The Kantian principle of universal hospitality is based on the ideal of a 'cosmopolitan right' as 'the natural right to visit' and as a right that allows mankind to circulate on a worldwide scale. For many people, this has acquired the meaning of an accessible reality, and sometimes – at least in those global circles that advocate a non-national right – the sense of a right that is enforceable from almost anywhere in the world. The ability to move around and to share one and the same world has become technically achievable. All that now remains is to make it politically applicable and acceptable to all 'by virtue of their common ownership of the earth's surface; for since the earth is a globe, they cannot scatter themselves infinitely, but must, finally, tolerate living in close proximity, because originally no one had a greater right to any region of the earth than anyone else' – as Kant famously put it.[7] If such a principle may have appeared utopian under the uncontested regime of national territorial powers, it is re-emerging today, not as a replacement for the previous 'reality' but in conflict with it. The cosmopolitan horizon described by Kant is, moreover, not unrealistic in the absolute. His proposal encompasses three highly significant ideas, all of which are a strikingly pertinent. First of all, as has already been noted, because the earth is round and because we will always encounter each other on 'the earth's surface', we have no choice but to get on with each other. Secondly, freedom of movement is the condition of being 'citizens of the world', given the need to cross borders in order to experience the world and other people, to reach beyond ourselves and the limits of our assigned identity. Finally, as Kant also states, exchanges, and especially commercial exchanges, will work better on a worldwide scale.

As the sociologist Ulrich Beck made clear, there is an epistemological conflict between 'methodological cosmopolitanism' and 'methodological nationalism'.[8] The significance of this distinction becomes clear when hospitality is examined in the context of its various 'scales' of meaning – domestic, local, national or global. Yet I would also like to emphasise that this conflict is as much political as epistemological. This is evident from the amount of space it takes up in national public debates and in the electoral choices made by European citizens over the course of recent years. But it is evident, too, when we look at this often observed contradiction between the cosmopolitan individual who is at the root of the political, revolutionary utopia of a cosmopolitical project and the impossible cosmopolitan nation, an oxymoron difficult to transpose onto a political horizon. We could say therefore that, if Kant is 'politically' cosmopolitan, he is 'epistemologically' nationalist. This is why, ultimately, the cosmopolitics he proposes take the form of an agreement between the nation-states and 'the form adopted [in his *Perpetual Peace*] is a parody of the diplomatic texts of his time'.[9] Today, in the twenty-first century, it is possible to reconsider this balance of power between citizens and the nation-states in the face of the need for a world politics. But we will need to keep this 'diplomacy' of international relations in mind when we try to imagine what form the principle of hospitality will take in the current configuration.

Furthermore, it is through this link between epistemology and politics that we can understand, conversely, the 'invisibility' of migrants as subjects of political debate despite the fact that they are strikingly overrepresented in the media (if we measure this representation in terms of their demographic significance, which is relatively small, particularly in France). And yet such politics, far from being absent, is evident on a daily basis. The protests and demands made by migrants are rarely transmitted, featured in the media, or 'carried' by national organisations, media groups, or politics. Yet there are a great many of them, and they focus on questions as essential to world politics as the right to emigrate, to remain in a chosen country, or to cross borders. Movements are born at the borders, at the roadblocks of Moria (on the island of Lesbos), of Idomeni (on the border between Greece and Macedonia), of Tijuana/ San Diego or Ciudad Juarez/El Paso (on both sides of the border between Mexico and the United States), of Ventimiglia (on the Italian–French border), and of Calais (on the British border in France). Chants and banners proclaim the right of entry, freedom of movement, respect for human rights, the recognition that we are all human and equal. Yet there is no capacity to render such movements meaningful and effective in terms of reflection or action on a national scale.

This interdependence between epistemology (how we describe reality) and politics (how reality is to be governed and transformed) is one of the key factors in any understanding of the political crisis that is being played out along national borders today. We will find it, below the surface, in the following discussion of the cosmopolitanism of philosophers. Such a discussion should enable us to clarify the terms and positions in a debate that is as much the concern of philosophy as it is of politics, law, and anthropology.

The question of cosmopolitanism takes us back, as I have said, to the Enlightenment. But philosophers, both today and in the past, speak to us rather of cosmo*politics*, sometimes under the name of cosmopolitanism, whereas in the approach taken in anthropology a distinction can be usefully made between the two terms. Cosmopolitical philosophy means envisaging, as Étienne Tassin did in following in the footsteps of the philosopher Hannah Arendt, the possibility of a 'common world' in a planetary context that would be shared by all humans, regardless of the social, spatial, and economic differences between them.[10] With this in mind, Tassin constructs an argument for a world politics based on the separation between globalisation and the common world, a separation that he analyses as 'the globalisation of the *acosmism*, a systemisation of the destruction of the world under cover of its economic and techno-scientific domination'.[11] Against this global 'governance' for which no alternative exists, Tassin sets out the idea that cosmopolitics is the permanent conflict between the 'acosmism' of globalisation and the quest for a common world. This introduces a certain amount of tension into Kant's overpacified vision, Tassin explains. Indeed, Kant's project for universal peace is marred by angelism, as is often pointed out, because it seems to have to be without conflict and without politics. Kant has left us an ethical standpoint, guidance on the best way of thinking of the world as it really is (without challenging its epistemological stato-national base). It is a vision that 'overlays' cosmopolitics (universal peace) onto cosmopolitanism, which he would summarise as 'inter-national' relations and which today takes on something of a 'politically correct' tone, inaudible and unrealistic in the face of the global 'realpolitik' of the nation-states. In his conception of cosmopolitics as conflict, Tassin leaves one question unresolved: that of the context and, more precisely, of the exact *locations* of cosmopolitics. It is indeed this question of location, of the space in which cosmopolitics is situated, that interests anthropologists and leads them to identify its new terrains. So what are the ethnographic and readily observable terrains where cosmopolitics is emerging?

In his book *Secularism and Cosmopolitanism*, Étienne Balibar also points out the similarity between the two notions – cosmopolitanism and cosmopolitics – while at the same time highlighting the anthropological specificity of a conflict that, here too, defines contemporary world politics, in the sense that it is itself constituted in relation to universalism: 'Contemporary cosmopolitics is a particularly ambiguous form of politics; it consists exclusively of conflicts between universalities without ready-made solutions [...] cosmopolitics clears the field for competition between *alternative* cosmopolitanisms.'[12] This cosmopolitics, formed out of conflicting universalisms, appears to lead straight to a relativist anthropology that describes competing truths: 'Truth on this side of the Pyrenees, error on the other side.' But, very differently, in the eyes of the anthropologist or of the poet, from the moment they have 'the whole world' in mind, this cosmopolitics of conflict also leads towards a genuine object of investigation: a cosmopolitan terrain, very far removed from any previously stated certainties. At this point we find ourselves entering the 'whole world' thinking of Édouard Glissant, and are reminded that this concept takes its origin in a social and cultural world historically marked by a series of encounters, crossroads, conflicts, blendings, and creolisations, to such an extent that it ended up generating the language of a cosmopolitan world: a language made up of 'globality' and of 'relation', of a sense of incompleteness and of permanent flux, and relevant to all on the basis simply of a single experience, that of the Caribbean Islands.[13] The field area of cosmopolitan anthropology involves situations made up of multiculturality (without multiculturalism necessarily being evoked), of many different languages, nationalities, geographical origins, and so on – all of which leads to the question: What social worlds form the contexts of *contemporary conflictual cosmopolitics*?

The earth has taken on a human scale. In the same way, as has been pointed out already, it has acquired an anthropological dimension by becoming the material form of universalism, its closest perimeter to date. This enables us, indeed urges us, to study the concrete forms of universalism as it is implemented, at the risk of seeing it disappear altogether. There are a great many situations of potential conflict, and each time they highlight the relativity of the universal. Reduced to one of the points of view available, or to becoming the focus of competing definitions, universalism is therefore very much dependent on the social form of the world: it becomes one of the issues at stake in the conflicts that make up cosmopolitics. It remains for us to know how to recognise and describe such situations.

Michael Fœssel and Louis Lourme succeed in edging closer to this *updating* of the cosmopolitical idea and to putting it to the test by calling for a social science of cosmopolitanism. First of all, they observe that, logically, the very idea of cosmopolitics seems to be an oxymoron, since it inevitably comes up against the incompatibility between the *political* scale (always local) and that of the *cosmos* (by definition global).[14] Today, this domain of politics is, from a normative point of view, national: parties, legislative assemblies, and executive authorities tend to be national (this is certainly the case in France, but less so in other countries, such as the independent regions of Spain or the federated states in Germany), and Europe itself is in fact stato-national. Put another way, the cosmopolitical ideal remains unrealistic as long as it does not have a political space of its own. Then Fœssel and Lourme observe that, in the contemporary world, *in reality*, 'global citizenship' is no longer (or not only) an idea or a stance but is in the process of becoming an 'unprecedented political reality', given that the nation-state 'is no longer alone in granting rights.[15] For the crisis of the nation-states, as described by Arendt in the 1950s, has deepened and, with the emergence of spaces for 'world rights', the question of non-national human rights has forced a breach in the area of rights. This is illustrated, for example, in the political problem of the 'stateless', already tackled by Arendt but which it is possible – and, in my view, pertinent today – to extend so as to include the cosmopolitan experience of international migrants, whoever they may be. Before coming back to this point, it is interesting to read one of the European polemics of the beginning of the twenty-first century as an illustration of this crisis in thinking concerning the links between individuals, the world, and the nation-states. It hinges on the polemical distinction, to be found practically in every single country, between those who are acknowledged to have rights ('refugees') and those who are not ('illegal immigrants') and who, because of this very word, 'illegal', remain defined as being outside the domain of rights in general.[16]

Finally and in an even broader sense, the authors note, to the detriment of a commanding ethical position, that 'cosmopolitanism has come to refer to an experience that is now more ordinary than used to be the case'.[17] They speak therefore of 'de facto cosmopolitanism' and, with reference to the ideas of the sociologist Ulrich Beck, of 'cosmopolitanism from below'.[18]

Banal cosmopolitanism: an anthropological point of view

Ultimately, this path leads us back to the reference to the 'terrain' or 'territory' of ordinary or banal cosmopolitan life, a fundamental preoccupation for anthropologists who take up this question as an object of research. In order to delimit this cosmopolitan terrain and to get to the core of the question, we need now to resolve some issues around definition, which should at the same time bring to an end a certain unease generated by the very word cosmopolitanism. Generally this word is associated with three different modes of living: most often it is used to refer to a globalised elite, which is both arrogant and distant; it is also the name adopted by a generally critical (alter-) globalist political movement; and, finally, it is used to describe a superior consciousness, the 'cosmopolitan consciousness'. Which of these three forms of cosmopolitanism are we referring to?

More often than not, then, the word 'cosmopolitan' is associated with a globalised way of life – the world of international experts, technocrats, leaders, and creators of images who speak of the world, of globalisation and who move around swiftly and smoothly, from one part of the planet to the other. From airports to planes and conference rooms, from identical shopping malls to smart hotel chains, they effectively live in a sort of global and culturally homogenous bubble, from which they rarely or never emerge and, from one capital city to the next, they travel around with very little physical effort on their part, flying across borders without even noticing, since they end up staying in more or less identical surroundings. Defined collectively, this group of people could be described as a global class insofar as they represent a social and cultural minority without locally rooted ethnicity and define themselves through contrast with those who could be described as 'local'.

In contrast with this global class, other people, generally grouped in protest movements and associations, see themselves as 'citizens of the world', or else as 'alter-globalists', as they were referred to in the 1990s, in the aftermath of the Cold War. These people would also describe themselves as 'cosmopolitans', but, to be more accurate, it will be observed that, in their case, this is already a matter of asserting a political position vis-à-vis the world and its governance that is largely representative, democratic or universalist. We are already in the realm of 'cosmo*politics*', where the philosophy of world politics has a role to play, as we have seen so far.

Finally, in a similar vein but moving from world politics to a somewhat less precise conception of the 'global society', Ulrich Beck, the sociologist of cosmopolitanism, believed that being cosmopolitan meant having a 'cosmopolitan consciousness'. He refers to the communal perception of shared risks, for example those related to health, which can occur at any point on the planet and simultaneously. This is the 'risk society': avian flu, tsunami, 11 September, terrorist attacks ...[19] On such occasions, appeals are being made to our consciousness from all directions at the same time. The sociological point of view becomes the norm when Beck argues that cosmopolitanism is a state of 'awareness' that challenges both the 'hierarchical subordination' between cultures and civilisations and the 'dissolution of differences'. The cosmopolitan individual would be someone who accepts differences, otherness, and the need for a power beyond the nation-state.

These three most widely accepted usages of the word and the concept of cosmopolitanism (global class, cosmopolitics, world consciousness) do not, however, really describe the cosmopolitan *condition* in the sense of something experienced in a day-to-day, ordinary way, an experience of the world no matter how unequal or how violent it may be. It is the experience of border situations in the broadest sense that, in my view, enables us to grasp another conception of cosmopolitanism. For my hypothesis is that cosmopolitanism is, first and foremost, a real and immediate experience of everything that pertains to a relationship with a near or distant outside and that therefore signals the 'world'. This is why the experience of migrants has for many years been the focus of at least some areas of the social sciences, in the sense that it is an experience where tensions between individuals, the nation-state, and cosmopolitics are played out in a very real way.

This ordinary experience of the world is that of borders and of crossing them. It can be protracted in time and in space. In these border situations there are moments, of varying duration, when any sense of identity is undermined by distance and by the experience of finding that the places, the bonds, and the belongings that made up identity have lost their meaning and their immediacy. And it is in such situations, too, that relationships with others – with the strangers who, for anyone who finds him- or herself in that situation, are also the embodiment of what the world represents – are put to the test. But in this context the border has a broad and anthropological meaning, which goes far beyond any stato-national and geopolitical definitions. It is situational in the sense that any particular experience brings into play geographical distinctions or separations (a city and its surrounding area, a closed-off area), or social ones (the numerous obstacles, differences, and clashes between different classes), or those relating to gender, religion, language, and culture in general. It is everything that, at a given time and place, separates, sets apart, and at the same time brings together – in a reciprocal glance, in a dispute, or in attempts to translate and to understand each other.[20]

Over the last twenty years or so, various social science research projects have highlighted what might be seen as the key role that migration plays in our understanding of the evolving nature of the world in general. In the mid-1990s, Nina Glick Schiller, along with Linda Basch and Cristina Szanton Blanc,[21] introduced the notion of 'transnational immigration', emphasising that migrants have roots in more than one society and that transnational life is an integral part of the day-to-day experience of both individuals and families of migrants. In France, the sociologist and ethnographer Alain Tarrius also saw 'transmigrants' and the poorest people among migrants as the bearers of a specific form of cosmopolitanism, which was developing its own networks and territories.[22] In Latin America, Gustavo Lins Ribeiro observed 'popular globalisation' in the course of his research on migrant street vendors in the city of Iguaçu, situated on the 'triple frontier' between Brazil, Argentina and Paraguay.[23] More generally, in the informal economy, Camille Schmoll describes the 'everyday cosmopolitanism' of the foreign small traders in Naples, where fragile commercial activities of varying degrees of legality mean that Italian, Algerian, Tunisian, Senegalese, Chinese, and Pakistani workers find themselves living side by side and meeting and interacting on a daily basis. Rejecting the external view (derived originally from politics or tourism) that it was a question of 'ethnic' circles or areas, thus generating an image that artificially homogenizes otherness and turns a blind eye to the cultural encounters that are played out on a daily basis, the geographer shows that those involved transform the way they act and think, and 'cultivate other links' than simply those associated with their group of origin. For her, these are 'cosmopolitan situations'.[24] Finally, Nina Glick Schiller has more recently taken her research on transnational migrants still further by asking the question: *Whose cosmopolitanism?*[25] And what contemporary social processes, what aspirations and desires does it encompass?

The exemplary nature of the cosmopolitanism observed among people on the move is not unique or exceptional, but simply the first indication of an ordinary world in the process of formation. Generally speaking, borders are more and more frequent because people leave their homes more often and because we can only see borders if we leave home. The challenge posed by human mobility is that it can only lead to an increase in border situations and ordinary cosmopolitanism. These are thresholds, made up of moments of transition, of crossovers and of uncertainties, places of encounter, of movement, of conflict, of relationships requiring translations and new types of exchange.

For the anthropologist, cosmopolitanism is an observable field area and a condition that is increasingly widespread in today's world. It involves living the experience of these border situations (crossings, obstructions, encounters, delays) with the accompanying social and cultural challenges. An ordinary, banal cosmopolitanism, which is most immediately, though not exclusively, exemplified by those caught up in migration (all sorts of migration, legal and illegal, for work, for study, for family reunification, as a means of escape or as part of a plan). In all these situations, we find ourselves brought face to face with the stranger. Far from disappearing, the stranger is now undeniably present on a global scale.

People move around, become more individualised, and with them comes an accompanying movement of ideas, of knowledge, of relationships, of ways of doing things, and so on. All this is played out and redefined at each new border situation in the broad sense. What the anthropologist sees in cosmopolitan situations is not the 'encounter of cultures', but instead people, real people, and he or she is part of such moments, since they are present in the situation being observed. Whatever their place of birth, the language they speak, or the colour of their skin, all these people are distinct individuals. They bring with them a unique and temporary cultural heritage of their own, the result of what they have learned and pieced together, and produce, *in real-life situations*, new cultural combinations that only the ethnologist will possibly want to describe as a whole, taking the intellectual liberty to determine the limits of this significant whole. But in such cases care must be taken not to 'essentialise' or naturalise the differences observed. Instead the ethnologist should set out to observe them as they go about their lives, capturing the dynamics of their daily activities, and in so doing ensure that these relational situations are seen against the background of their specific contexts, their biographies, the constraints that exist between them, the places themselves and the manner in which all these factors come together in any given situation.

A wide variety of choices confront the ethnologist in quest of a terrain from which to reach an understanding of the emergence of a cosmopolitics, even if he or she may subsequently be side-tracked, or to take a different direction. I am convinced that it is possible to see concrete demonstrations of the 'globalised' world in any field area whatsoever, regardless of how local and remote it may be.

One Tuesday evening in December 2017, at the end of a spoken presentation of these theoretical and methodological considerations given in one of the seminars on my course 'Anthropologies of Hospitality' at the *École des hautes études en sciences sociales* (School of Advanced Studies in the Social Sciences), at the point where I was inviting participants to give their comments, questions, or criticisms, a female student asked me if this analysis could be applied to the context of a youth hostel that might be regarded as a border situation and an example of a cosmopolitan field area. Initially amused by this suggestion, like other people present, I soon began to feel relieved and happy that I had succeeded in conveying a conception of cosmopolitanism and of borders broad enough to stimulate curiosity about potentially new terrains, such as the one cited on this occasion, which is undoubtedly a precursor of cosmopolitan ways of life. Yes, a youth hostel – an 'international residential and cultural centre' or a 'European residential centre', according to the definition more frequently in use today – can indeed be viewed through the prism of a border (in all possible senses of the word). Look, for example, at the issue of what language(s) are used for communication. More or less everybody speaks *globish* English,[26] but other languages can also be used as an alternative by small groups. Differences in behaviour, and certain understandings and misunderstandings depend just as much on social class as on nationality as factors likely to make people feel more or less at ease or else out of place. Certain potentially risky subjects (Syria, Palestine) are not immediately brought up in conversations in the youth hostel cited by my young interlocutor. Certain gender choices are compared and put into perspective, even if this sometimes happens in an atmosphere of irritation, of argument, or of conflict and in the end can lead to new habits of eating, of getting together, of working, and of relaxing. Of course, there is nothing essential about all this, but gradually, over time, the sense of national loyalty can end up shrinking in importance in comparison with an identification based on gender, linguistic proximity, professional interests, artistic tastes or skills, or the desire to travel or to settle down.

Although no more than an exercise, it is precisely an example such as this that enables us to recognise a meaningful situation, which merits comparison with other 'borders' and other cosmopolitan moments, places, and situations that operate on what might be much broader scales and involve much more serious challenges. In this way, might I venture to suggest, leaving aside poverty, anxiety about the future, and the lack of legal status, the conversations touched on here, which involved young people from Europe, Africa, and the Middle East temporarily brought together in a youth hostel, could just as easily be the conversations, games, jokes, arguments, and desires observed in the shanty town camp of the Calais 'jungle'.[27]

In order to answer the question of the impact that cosmopolitanism has on politics, we must turn our attention to the cosmopolitan field. The 'conflict of universalisms' cannot be regarded as fieldwork data as such. It is an external interpretation, indeed a commanding one, driven by media and politics and based on the acceptance of the idea that there are fixed forms of cultural identity attributed to the names of groups, of nationalities, of ethnicities, forms that will be imposed on each person, in a sense wiping out the notion of individual subjects and serving only to confirm the powerful divisions in terms of identity already established in the world. In reality, the border situations that are perceived as tests of cosmopolitanism are a setting for a whole range of identify games, played out for the purpose of sharing spaces and roles in each new situation. But beyond these different identities and cultures constantly in the process of being reconfigured and transformed, one fact remains constant and is undeniably the most universal: each of these situations turns a spotlight on, and for a while re-creates, one or more representations of the stranger. The subsequent welcome or rejection, the coming together or distancing, indifference, tolerance, violence – will all depend on such combinations of continuously reconstructed experiences and representations. By exploring this final question – how does someone become a stranger? – I want to avoid losing sight of the central issue, raised at the start of this discussion: How does the stranger end up as my guest – or, for that matter, as my enemy?

4

Becoming a Stranger

There are many different ways of becoming a stranger, and we can rejoice first of all for the relativity which dissolves the being (*ser* in Spanish and Portuguese) into the being-in-the-world (*estar*) and allows us to challenge any notions of essentialism or 'identitarianism' attached to the stranger and to his or her host, by freeing us all, methodologically at least, from any belief in such absolutes.

How does someone become a stranger? (1) By arriving from somewhere else, from the outside, and, even without meaning to, disturbing an established order of place, whatever form that might take – house, village, district, housing project, town, region, state. This is the exteriority of the stranger as someone who comes from outside, someone who is an outsider. (2) By crossing an administrative, institutional, or legal border. This is the extraneity of the stranger (the *foreigner*), who needs rights in order to make progress, through a series of gradual steps, towards obtaining citizenship. (3) By leaving behind everything that is familiar and discovering a different world, in which everything must be learned all over again. This is the relative strangeness of the *stranger*. (4) Finally, we should remember that there can also be a state that is 'radically' other, in other words that goes to the very 'root' of otherness (root, *radix* in Latin, the origin of 'radical') and seems almost at the very limit of what is human, as though alienated to a different world altogether and therefore rendered invisible, moving into the realm of fiction, of science fiction even. This is the radicalism of the absolute stranger (the *alien*).

Before revisiting and exploring each of these ways of being (and of being considered to be) a stranger, let us turn our attention to a story about a stranger. It is an old story, rooted in history, and therefore one that can help us to reflect on the past and take a 'calmer' view of an issue that has become so contentious. And it is a story that provides us with a common thread with which to decipher the different aspects of the stranger in general. Let us examine, then, the case of Stavros the stranger.

The death of Stavros or the birth of Joe Arness

For twenty years or so, he lives where he was born, with his Greek family, in Anatolia, at the end of the nineteenth century. In the Ottoman Empire the Turks are in power and violently repress Greek and Armenian minorities who struggle for survival. As a result, young Stavros decides to leave. He thinks of going to America, which in his eyes is a land of peace, freedom, and economic success. His father wants to help him leave, but favours the idea of the capital, Constantinople. He gives his son all the money he can, as well as the address of a cousin who, he says, will help Stavros and find him work. For Stavros, the city is the gateway to America.

Tricked in the early days by someone he had met on the road and robbed of all his father's savings, Stavros ends up sleeping rough on the roadside and, later, on the pavements of Constantinople. Between the worlds of work, of the street, and of the family, he makes friends, finds romance, and eventually manages to secure a place on a ship. On arrival at Ellis Island, everything changes dramatically in the biography of Stavros, paternal uncle to Elia Kazan – the American film director who would later, in 1963, transform this tale into an epic saga with the film *America, America*.

On Ellis Island, the emigrants wait to be transformed into immigrants, which, at that key moment at the beginning of the twentieth century, means becoming American. But, in order for that to happen, they need to prove that they are both physically healthy and morally sound. During the voyage Stavros had found himself in serious trouble, and this now threatens to jeopardise his right to enter the new country; but he has kept shoes and papers belonging to a friend, one Hohanness, who died during the journey. On arrival, he mingles with a group of people who had been friends with Hohanness and were on board, having been recruited in Constantinople by an American gangmaster in search of labour. In that queue on Ellis Island, he no longer has either a name or an identity. He is, as it were, in a state of limbo, his fate hanging on the identity he will be given. Then comes that famous scene, the pivotal moment in the film and, more broadly, a defining moment in the condition of the stranger. The police officer asks the group: 'Stavros… Any of you go by that name?' The reply follows: 'He died last night.' Then, signalling Stavros to approach, the police officer says to him: 'You, what's your name?' The gangmaster replies: 'Hohanness.' Stavros, too, reiterates: 'Hohanness.' To which the policeman's reply is: 'Wanna be an American? The first thing you need to do, is to change that name.' Stavros repeats 'Hohanness, Hohanness.' After a moment's thought, the police officer is heard to say: 'Hohanness? Well, OK. Let's make that "Joe Arness"! How does that suit you?' And Stavros, wreathed in smiles and triumphant replies: 'Joe …

Arness?! Hohanness, Joe Arness, yes, Joe Arness, Joe Arness.' 'Well Joe, you're reborn. You're baptised again without the clergy.' A few moments later, his feet are treading the soil of New York, which he stoops to kiss. American citizen and shoeshine boy, Stavros/Joe Arness will end up gradually bringing all his family to join him in America.

It is that moment when he is no longer anything that I would like to fix in memory, those few minutes in the life of Stavros. A moment we scarcely pay attention to, so short and subtle is it. Nothing happens, only the waiting and the uncertainty about who he is and what he is to become. Yet in reality the experience of Stavros highlights a number of aspects of what it means to become a stranger; and I shall re-examine and discuss these in more detail.

Three times a stranger

For Stavros, home is Anatolia, even if the place is occupied and controlled by Turks, who have turned his people into a minority group and made them lesser citizens. He feels attachment to this place, like the rest of his family, but life has become untenable and he must move on. It is by leaving his home that he will begin to be an *outsider*, someone who comes from elsewhere. It will be many years before he reaches America, and everywhere he goes he will continue to be an *outsider* and will be perceived as such, from the very first village he passes through (where he is robbed of all his money) to Constantinople, where he spends a good deal of time drifting, and then all the way to New York and the soil of that city, which he reaches in a very physical sense as he crosses the ship's gangway. Much later, the film producer Elia Kazan – who had, himself, arrived in the United States in 1913, at the age of four and been welcomed by this uncle, 'Joe Arness' – would acknowledge that somewhere deep inside he had always had the feeling of having come from elsewhere, of being an outsider.[1]

And yet this newly arrived stranger, the *outsider*, is, first of all, simply the name for a state of *exteriority*; he or she embodies mobility in general (the journey, the world) and an indeterminate 'outside'. It is this use of the term that is undoubtedly the most frequently used today with reference to someone who comes from elsewhere and whom we do not yet know, as opposed to my guest, whom I already know or who was introduced to me by people I am close to. The outsider often describes him- or herself by referring to a geographical image that can sometimes become dehumanising with its emphasis on a state of flux, on waymarks and spatial limits. Such a definition implies exteriority, and yet this external aspect of the stranger is visible only because he or she is at the border and is therefore well and truly present: indeed the outsider is defined in relation to the one who is already established – together they define a situation that will involve all sorts of different borders. But the notions of space, place, and territory must be called upon first of all. In the most technical way possible, it might be said that the stranger who turns up is an 'intruder' who, like a foreign body, imposes his or her presence on top of the established arrangement of things, places, and people. The stranger needs to find a place in a pre-existing local order. We can say once again, with Jean-Luc Nancy, that we would be wrong to deny the person this intrusion, which immediately and unequivocally renders him or her a stranger, since it 'insists': 'Something of the stranger has to intrude.'[2] for without it, he or she loses some of that exteriority. For the person who is settled somewhere those who are in the process of arriving are seen as strangers, as outsiders. The mystery surrounding them is complete and nobody knows from which country or which neighbouring village they have come, what their cultural background is, what language they speak ('Hohanness?' the police officer says). And this stranger, the one who is my guest is, for his part, the one who is, and will have been even if only once, this intruder, someone who will forever retain a physical, linguistic, social, psychological, remembered trace of their exteriority.

The identity-based version of geography exacerbates this definition of the stranger – which might appear to be the most neutral one – by linking it to territory and to the fiction of autochthony. On all sides there are conflicting references to the territorial affiliation of some and the physical intrusion of others, and these draw on naturalising and biologising elements: between 'autochthons' (original inhabitants of the land)' and 'foreigners' according to the terms used in Europe: between 'indigenous peoples' and 'settlers' in the history of the Americas, or between 'autochthons' and *allogènes* (meaning non-natives, those originating from other gene pools) in West Africa today. The historical contexts are different, and sometimes the same words can be given the opposite political meaning – for example the notion of being a native in Europe and in North and South America. The complexity increases as mobility starts to expand throughout the world and all of us find ourselves confronted with this status of outsider. We are increasingly becoming strangers in the world, that is to say, *outsiders*, even if we are not so in reality – not all of us, and especially not in the same manner – when it comes to the two other dimensions of becoming a stranger, namely the legal and the cultural dimensions.

A second conception of the stranger relates to belonging or, more precisely, to *lack of belonging*.[3] This is the absence of affiliation to any particular family group or clan, such as a village community, a province, a city, or a specific national state, and it is this that determines the stranger's varying degree of *extraneity* as a foreigner. When Stavros leaves his Anatolian village, his father provides him with the address of a cousin who, he says, will find Stavros work in Constantinople. The family connections that he finds in the city offer him resources, somewhere to stay, access to a social world, and a few relatives to whom he is connected through his own genealogy. As a result of all this, he feels a little less of a stranger in this city, where he is a new arrival. According to the largely autobiographical story retold by Elia Kazan, Stavros is not utterly lost, no longer really a stranger, since his uncle in Constantinople is able to offer him hospitality. Acting as a father figure, he wants to marry Stavros to a young woman close to the family, an arrangement that will at the same time bring him a respectable job and strengthen his uncle's position in the city's commercial circles. But the young man wishes to remain independent and is reluctant to bow to his uncle's authority. He hesitates, but in the end refuses the wife his uncle has in mind. He then becomes the lover of a rich Greek émigrée who has returned to her home country for a holiday, before leaving for the United States with her American husband. It is she who enables Stavros to board a vessel bound for America. And in the end, it is thanks to another group with which he forms an affiliation that he ends up being saved on arrival, even though serious problems with his mistress and her husband while on board the ship could have prevented him from achieving his goal. Through his association with this new group of itinerants (encountered in the streets of Constantinople), he will make contact with an American gangmaster who will find him work in New York as a shoeshine boy. Stavros, who has become the Uncle Joe of the Anatolian family, will himself become the hub of a social network and

will play host to all the various family members he will
end up sending for.

The condition of being a stranger, which is determined by extraneity, is adjustable and flexible. This is
evident in the different ways in which Stavros establishes a sense of belonging at different times in his
journey; and it is also evident in the research carried
out by the historian Simona Cerutti on the archives
of the city of Turin in the seventeenth and eighteenth
centuries (when the city was still part of the Savoyard
states). The stranger, according to her, is a condition,
not an individual or an identity. It is a 'provisional
condition' in the life of an individual and depends on
his or her degree of extraneity, in other words on the
extent to which that individual is 'a stranger to a social
order and to the authority that controls it', or a stranger
to a village-based or urban 'community'. Extraneity,
from a legal point of view, amounts to the various
rules that determine the rights accorded to strangers in
the host country. It hinges on the access that strangers
might have to the rights of a place where they cannot
claim nationality: civil rights, property rights, the right
to work. We know that, depending on the country,
some of these rights exist and others do not. The 'lack
of belonging' varies according to a scale defined by
the fact of having certain rights and duties in the eyes
of those who fully belong, those with citizens' rights.
Such strangers, adds Simona Cerutti, are not necessarily 'people living on the fringes', nor do they 'wear
the mask of the Other or of the one who is different':
they are simply individuals whose status as citizens is
incomplete.[4] That could be a neighbour from the village
or someone from the neighbouring province. It could
be, for example, someone from the Cevennes arriving
in one of the Savoyard kingdoms and being regarded as
a stranger (this is the seventeenth century after all): one
of the elements that indicated his condition as a stranger

at that time was the possibility of a *droit d'aubaine* accorded to the prince vis-à-vis any foreigners. This right allowed the prince to seize for himself any goods belonging to a foreigner who died on his land. It was the responsibility of the administrative process to assess the extent to which the foreigner in question was extraneous to the host province (if he or she was bound by any family links, for example), or else to attempt to track down any creditors likely to claim their share of this inheritance; and, once these checks had been completed, the foreigner's goods and possessions were made over to the government of the province in which he or she had died. The historian therefore asks: Exactly what distance was implied by the term 'foreigner' in the societies of that time? There would thus be a gradation of rights in any specific political context. In the Savoyard states of the seventeenth and eighteenth centuries, this gradation was defined by the absence of access to property, to succession, to work, and so on.

The key question concerns the potential for integration, in other words the possibility of finding space for the stranger within the social body. This is the sense conveyed by the English word *foreigner*, as I have already pointed out, and also by the Spanish *forastero* and by the old French *forain*. In old French, the latter was used to describe the 'stranger in the village', the 'person who is not from here' – and, later, in *le marchand forain*, the itinerant pedlar. Belonging is not merely a matter of legal rights, but rather refers to rights of *all kinds*, considered from a more broadly sociological point of view, that of the stranger's place in the existing social organisation. Take for example the trader, like those described in research on long-distance trading in precolonial Africa. Here the person who did not belong to a social group was the one who could be involved in trading, in that he stood out from the village communities as someone passing through. He could trade because he was not involved in the local exchange cycles, not part of the system of gift and counter-gift, and therefore able to receive money for the objects he supplied. This is an essential element in the existence of societies and could also be organised within the context of a diaspora. The trading diasporas are, in a sense, foreigners organised in a transnational manner. Their autonomy becomes the basis for their separate social organisation. This foreigner, male or female, is also, in many instances in Western Africa, the person who represents exogamy and enables lineage to be renewed through the process of sending for, or accepting, a marriage partner from outside the clan. There is indeed a relationship between the stranger or the foreigner and the social group to whom he or she is effectively a foreigner. Being a foreigner does not imply the absence of any relationships. Marrying outside the clan, trading outside the cycle of exchanges, taking on certain specific professions were all indications of the fact that, in precolonial Africa just as in Turin under the ancien régime, there was a need for this stranger, for the foreigner.

Finally, this 'trader as stranger' is, according to the sociologist Georg Simmel, the most urbane and the most modern representation of all, given that, although he may indeed have arrived yesterday and could still be here tomorrow, he has not lost the freedom to come and go as he pleases. This freedom can form a distinct culture of its own, in other words it can become the ethos of the stranger: it is a case where a condition can, in a sense, be transformed into a culture – and I shall return to this a little later. But let us for the moment continue to focus on extraneity, this particular aspect of the condition of being a stranger that we have looked at from a legal and from a political perspective. Simmel, for his part, refers to the 'sociological form of the "stranger,"' a form that represents both mobility and freedom.[5] This is, in a way, the positive side of that 'lack of belonging' that has been discussed here. Furthermore, in this case the stranger is no longer on the outside at all, but instead occupies an integral role in that society. He is part of it; but, as a 'potential wanderer', a position unique to the stranger, he remains part of the group, yet someone whose affiliation (or lack of affiliation) takes the form of an apparent exteriority, or of some trace of exteriority. Even more, Simmel explains that the fact that he is not 'bound up organically' (through ties of kinship, locality, occupation) guarantees the 'objectivity of the stranger'.[6] And Simmel, too, takes the example of certain Italian cities 'recruiting their judges from outside, because no native was free from entanglement in family interests and factionalism,' in order to pass judgement in complete objectivity and complete freedom. Objective, free, intermediary, neutral, the unique participation of the stranger resembles 'the objectivity of a theoretical observation', the sociologist even suggests. Always somewhat on the outside of things, the stranger therefore occupies a position of knowledge by taking the place of an observer, on the edges and at the limits, a position that brings with it certain risks. The stranger can always be considered as the emissary for the interests of strangers in general. We begin to see the interconnection with the cultural and anthropological dimension of the stranger as a *stranger*, to which I would now like to turn my attention.

When he first arrives in Constantinople, the young Stavros is disorientated and physically awkward, and stands out because of his appearance and his village clothes. But he learns quickly and, a few sequences later, we see him as a labourer, toiling away to save money for his journey, then as a handsome city dweller, elegant in his fashionable clothes and hairstyle, and finally, for a few moments, as an American, joyful and ambitious: a young working man once again, but a New Yorker and speaking English with a strongly oriental accent. Throughout his journey, Stavros looks at the world with an exaggeratedly wide-eyed gaze; it is as though this is what Elia Kazan intended, urging the actor to convey surprise, a sense of discovery, of new experiences, and of resourcefulness. This sense of discovery and its many implications represents a third element in the definition of the stranger, this time an anthropological one: the cultural other. This element is revealed by what might be called an interethnic or intercultural relationship. It suggests otherness and corresponds to the double strangeness inherent in the English word 'stranger', my own strangeness to others and that of others to me. Put in a different way, it refers to everything that is not familiar to us: 'people are strange when you are a stranger.' If we look beyond the linguistic or ethnic differences, we find all the dimensions of 'relative strangeness' – which can be considered as an active, evolving way of referring to cultural otherness. This is never fixed once and for all. Referring to the strangeness of the stranger means grasping otherness as a discovery and as an opportunity to learn about everything previously unknown to me.[7]

I would like very briefly to mention another New York-related example, to which I have previously referred elsewhere.[8] It is one inspired by the Jewish Austrian sociologist Alfred Schütz, exiled in July 1939 to the United States, where he would settle with his family and remain until his death twenty years later. He would draw on his own experience as a sociologist and as an émigré to reflect on the phenomenology of the stranger, that is, on the adjustments, interpretations, and learning processes that the stranger experiences at every level. Schütz pays close attention to the way in which cultural models intersect and superimpose themselves, partly in order to generate a new way of 'thinking as usual' that is syncretic and unique. For the stranger arrives into a new situation, which he or she discovers by thinking about it in a way that seems self-evident and natural to him or her, and must then learn to navigate in a 'new cultural pattern (language, customs, laws, folklore, fashions, etc.), which needs to be understood in order to be put to use. This is the image of the stranger in a labyrinth. In order to keep this image of the otherness of the stranger without reducing it to a previously attributed ethnic identity, but trying instead to generalise and universalise it, the best definition of this strangeness might indeed be that of a labyrinth, of having to understand a new place and of learning to live and behave according to its rules. As a result of this ordeal, the stranger acquires two fundamental traits: on the one hand, objectivity and a 'conception of the world' – he or she has discovered that 'the normal way of life is always far less guaranteed than it seems'; on the other hand, a 'doubtful loyalty', one that is reticent or incapable of completely substituting one cultural model for another: the stranger is a 'cultural hybrid on the verge of two different patterns of group life, not knowing to which of them he belongs'.[9] Such challenges are far more numerous today than at the time when sociologists like Schütz and Simmel found themselves musing in this way. In a context that is increasingly cosmopolitan, where everybody is in some way involved, the balance between strangeness and familiarity represents a frequently encountered challenge. From the 'contact situations' studied by ethnologists in the colonial era we have moved on today, in the increasingly globalised world, to a state where border situations have gradually become far more widespread. It is as though we were still in the process of discovering something that is strange to us, someone who is a stranger to us.

It might be assumed that the question of cultural strangeness has changed since the 1940s, when Alfred

Schütz was writing. It might also be possible to try to identify what these changes might be, while confining oneself strictly to the domain of interactions between strangers, in the manner of the two sociologists referred to here and with reference to their phenomenology of strangeness. First, communications have improved and developed, and this means increased access to information about other people; but with it comes a rise in false information about others and the challenge of having to distinguish between truth and fiction in terms of what those others actually represent. Secondly, there is a growing awareness of the significant role played by language learning and translation. Increasingly we are seeing the dominance of a few linguae francae to the detriment of local, vernacular languages. With regard to these dominant languages we need to take a broad view. As well as English, there is also Swahili in Eastern Africa, Hausa in Central and Western Africa, and Dyula even further west. Then there is Spanish, and also the language called Spanglish, associated with Latin American migrants to the United States, and finally Globish, which comes under criticism from the philosopher Barbara Cassin.[10] For Cassin, who loves languages and their diversity, we need more translation and less Globish. I do not think we will manage to stop completely this generic English, this 'global English', from becoming the primary linguistic vehicle – in the sense that it facilitates travel. Thirdly, it is also true that we increasingly recognise the importance and even the central role of mediation and mediators, of linguistic translators as well as of cultural translators in explaining a particular cultural difference between one place and another, and, of course, of 'social interpreters' – this is how I describe social workers, since they are also the mediators of this increasingly interwoven world. These are the most recent and, in my view, the most significant changes that are currently in the process of transforming the cultural dimension of the condition of being a stranger.

The migrant poet and the spectre of the alien

These three definitions of the stranger – exteriority, extraneity, strangeness – are linked therefore to three different kinds of borders – geographical, sociopolitical, and cultural – all of which we regularly encounter in the course of our lives. And we have seen how the relative and fluctuating nature of these borders depends on different contexts. Let us therefore advance the hypothesis that the condition of stranger, which all of us will experience in our lives for varying lengths of time, provisionally or more permanently – a condition to which our identities cannot be reduced but which is nevertheless a hybrid part of them – is a combination, always individual, of these three 'elements', each of which is subject to variation and change.

Let us now imagine that each of the three elements functions as an axis and that there is a cursor that can be moved up or down, from extraterritorial confinement (low) to the opening up of spaces (high) in terms of exteriority, from the total lack of any rights of belonging (low) to full rights of citizenship (high) from the perspective of extraneity, from extreme invisibility in terms of existence and culture (low) to a full recognition and understanding by and with others (high) in terms of strangeness. The level of intensity, positive or negative, of each of these three concepts, and the interaction between them, are what determines and puts into perspective the perceptions, contexts, and treatments of each stranger in our contemporary world.

If all three cursors are pushed towards the top of each axis, the result would be the good and happy life of any citizen of the world anywhere on earth; it is a life that no one has yet experienced but one that can be imagined, one that would be the concrete realisation of this cosmopolitan utopia championed since the Enlightenment and referred to here. All individuals can situate themselves as they see fit, and according to their own experiences, at one level or another on each of the three axes of the condition of stranger: feeling more or less at home, having greater or lesser access to civil rights, and encountering greater or lesser cultural recognition anywhere on earth. But if each individual can thus 'climb' closer to this transformation from stranger to cosmopolitan citizen, each can just as easily find him- or herself descending the axis. What I am seeking to suggest, with this visual image of an axis and cursors, is that we are not necessarily projected into a different world when the three cursors plummet together to the lowest point of the axis and thus form the exact opposite but symmetrical image to that of cosmopolitan happiness – in other words the image of the absolute stranger, invisible, stripped of any rights and trapped at the border.

Let us come back to Stavros one last time, to that moment I have already described in which he becomes a *pure stranger*, when, in the Ellis Island queue, at the very instant when he is about to reply to the police officer, he has lost his name and has not yet been given a new one. For a few seconds, Stavros is this absolute stranger, stripped of any identity. This brief moment of inexistence, suspended in the wait for the papers that, complete with the stamp and signature, would open the border for him, is a fleeting one in his case. But it is an experience we find again today, and lasting much longer, on migrant routes in very many different locations around the world. Held up and abandoned without any rights at borders and on sea crossings, on mountain or desert routes, people are forced to interrupt their journeys for periods often much longer than the few moments that separated the death of Stavros from the birth of Joe Arness. Much longer indeed, but no different in nature. This long period of indeterminacy experienced at the very limit of the stranger's existence is described in another film, *Spectres Are Haunting Europe*,[11] where we see the same people coming and going on either side of the Macedonian–Greek border at Idomeni. They drift in one direction and then back the opposite way, in front of a fixed camera, before returning and then setting off again, until it is clear that they are going nowhere. Other shots show them sitting on the railway lines, gathering on tracks where no trains ever come, talking and protesting. Later on, the camera focuses on the faces of these people, weary, expressionless faces, yet always smiling in front of the tents. The tent has become home to the stranger waiting to move on, and in particular the Quechua tent – which catches our attention because it is the one we associate with a hike and an overnight camp at the weekend, or with a few days' escape from the city – has become the border tent, the migrant's tent, and is often part of a much more extensive encampment. Tents like these, temporary campsites like these, even in a more makeshift form (and a lower position of the cursor on the axis of rights), with plastic tarpaulin thrown over stakes, can be found in the Ta'ang region, on the border between Myanmar and China.[12] Here there is nothing but immobility, waiting, and uncertainty – and women saying: 'We should never have come here, we'll never be able to leave.' In both these cases, in the Ta'ang region and at Idomeni,[13] it is perfectly possible to shoot long films at the border itself, whereas at the beginning of the twentieth century the border featured for just a few minutes in the course of the long film *America America*. Today there is excessive focus on the border and on that particular moment of crossing it, which is marked by an effacement of any previous identity. What, then, is a stranger who remains at the border? An outsider left on the outside, a foreigner who has hit rock bottom in terms of civil rights, how does he deal with his cultural strangeness as a stranger? All that is left is a generalised form of the stranger, anonymous, lacking any distinguishing features, slowly descending into oblivion.

It is at this point that a fourth figure emerges, a sort of spectre or fantasy, not unlike the fictional depiction of the *alien*. The aesthetic and political imagination constructs the alien as an absolute and radical other. Yet this other is in fact merely ourselves, at the lowest point in terms of a right to free movement, of the recognition of civil rights, of cultural relationships.

That stranger is not absent from the world of ideas and of images. On the one hand, we find him or her in the English use of the word 'alien', formerly taken to suggest simply an 'ethnic' other, but now radicalised by the migratory conflict through its association with clandestinity: this is the illegal alien, the illegal stranger. On the other hand, the stranger is to be found in the French understanding of the English word 'alien': the extraterrestrial of science fiction films, the one who, it is said, is coming closer to us, the earthlings, and seeking to establish 'contact'. In that case it would be the more generic image of an alien belonging to another world, another universe.

The alien is a fictional invention. The anxiety it conceals is heightened in the present moment because of our collective failure to envisage mobility for all, along with the right to belong and be recognised. Somewhere deep inside this fiction, or at the lowest depths of this descent into the subhuman, lurks the spectre of racial assignation that will in a sense be the preferred mechanism for its implementation, its 'reification'. So, for example, the police officers patrolling the borders at Ventimiglia know that they must distinguish between, on the one hand, those who live close to the border, or tourists, who can circulate freely (since the city is in the Schengen area), and, on the other, the undesirable migrants or the illegal aliens, halted in their onward journey and trapped between two border posts. In addition to the faces themselves – necessary but not sufficient, since in a Mediterranean city there could easily be confusion between the resident, the tourist, and the vagabond – the border police must also be able to recognise the body of the undesirable stranger. In this operation, which at each moment constantly reinforces the link between the biological and the social, the police are drawing upon the full extent of western postcolonial knowledge of racial otherness. The ancient perceptions of Africanism and orientalism are played out again, in a contemporary version, for the purposes of police identification.

The alien is also a fiction in that it refers to someone who is socially undesirable but can be economically useful. For, in the ideal form of capitalism without any constraints (so-called neoliberal), the absolute stranger in this particular representation, as socially undesirable, without any rights, belonging nowhere and unrecognised, constitutes an available workforce that of course imposes no social costs except the humanitarian one of minimum survival, or indeed of 'natural' selection in favour of the most resourceful. The stranger in the form of the worker with no security, no papers, no rights, and no fixed address is thus the first of us to experience a lesser humanity, since he or she discovers what it means when the notion of human rights 'for all' is called into question, according to the criticism of this 'rights of man-ism', which is today widely espoused by ideologues of the right throughout the world.

This nameless stranger does not exist. If I have equated this stranger to the notion of the alien, it is in order to make a clear analytical distinction and to contribute to an understanding of the imaginary realm that lies hidden behind the public policies and the words of fear and national hostility towards the stranger – permanently perceived as an intruder and whose intrusion must be prevented or meticulously contained. Reality is altogether different, and yet it is built around the notion of this spectre, as though this represented some kind of double with whom reality must constantly do battle.

It was after reading an article written by a journalist he had encountered at the Porte de La Chapelle, north of Paris, that Hassan Yacine was inspired to 'respond' by writing 'La Malédiction' ('The Curse'), a poem he then circulated among his friends and acquaintances.[14] The article, entitled 'One Kilometre of Garbage', described the situation in the migrant camp set up below the overground metro line between the stations of La Chapelle and Stalingrad. In a tent under the metro, Yacine writes his poems without paper, in the very spot from where they are then distributed on a smartphone that turns out to be not much of a *phone* but much else besides.

> Give me a light so I can burn my garbage
> I am a decaying corpse filling your air with foul
>   stench
> Forcing you to detest your slender bodies
> Perfumed with the floral scents of Paris
> I fill you with hatred for the human race
> My broken fellow creatures
> Who have endured the horrors of wars

Hassan is the embodiment of all that is meant by the 'migrant crisis' in Europe. In charge of an NGO set up to help the destitute in Khartoum, he was subject to harassment and thrown into prison for forty-five days by the Sudanese government, which accused him of portraying a negative image of his country, particularly since he had previously had contacts with international organisations that placed too much emphasis on human rights. He had worked for a while for the Belgian branch of Médecins sans Frontières (Doctors without Borders) before setting up his own organisation.

From Khartoum he headed northwards, to Egypt, reaching Cairo, where he spent several days before heading west to Libya, making his way along the coast, through towns such as Tobruk, he recalls, and others that he simply passed through, until finally a small boat took him to Sicily.

> I am a migrant who has survived the rotting of flesh
> In the Mediterranean
> Only to end up rotting in the streets of Paris
> These streets that are cleaned at dawn ... unlike me!

In Sicily and in the rest of Italy, he managed to avoid ending up in a detention centre by escaping from the bus that was taking him to one of them while it was stopped, and slipping away along with a handful of others. He walked for a long time, reaching Rome, and from there made his way to Turin and, finally, to Ventimiglia. Throughout his journey he was helped by 'collectives' and by people who welcomed him into their own homes. He crossed the border at Ventimiglia by using lesser known roads with the help of Google Maps, having found €10 that enabled him to connect to the internet. Hassan is strong. He manages to get through even when other people tell him: 'You won't make it.' He got to Nice, where he was provided with somewhere to stay and helped by various associations, and finally reached Paris on 6 April 2016. He spent a month in various camps in the capital, then a week in the Calais 'jungle'. Referring to this experience, he had this to say: 'So many people, all so different, are managing to live together, normally, in peace. There are arguments, but only over ordinary things like problems

with money, food, water, and not about religion or
nationality.'

In Paris he began the process of applying for asylum.
He was housed in a number of different flats by the
social services. For several months he cohabited with
a Chechen couple and ended up speaking Russian,
then with Armenians and Iranians. Each time, with a
certain amount of amusement, he ended up learning
the language and the customs of his co-residents. But
it is French that he really wants to learn, though he
has not so far succeeded in finding a way to make this
happen. 'I absolutely must speak French', says the poet
of Khartoum, who can recite Baudelaire and Verlaine
and whose eyes light up at the mention of Baudelaire.

After many months, he obtained an interview with an
official at the Office français de protection des réfugiés et
apatrides (OFPRA; The French Office for the Protection
of Refugees and Stateless Persons) with a view to having
his request for asylum examined. She refused to give
him the key to freedom represented by the right to
asylum because, so he was told, 'you have lied'. Not
enough prison, even though it was forty-five days, not
enough police harassment, not enough funding cuts
to his association, no tangible evidence (photos, statements) of his fate as a teacher and activist. He wrote a
poem, 'Les Menteurs' ('The Liars'), the opening lines of
which are addressed to this all-powerful woman: 'Dear
Madame'. Hassan has adopted the habit of using his
poetry to respond to aggression. It is poetry that allows
him to explain that he lives with fear, his 'secret friend',
as he describes it in the opening lines of his poem 'The
Curse':

> I am a curse
> I am the curse personified
> Dangling from my secret cord
> Attached to the uterus of the sky

I hear the cries of the wind and weeping all around
I speak to the flowers surrounding me and admire the
     song of the walls
These walls of my endless isolation
And Fear is my secret friend
Nothing can bring me a sense of safety

Hassan the poet's request for asylum was turned down.
He moved from one place to another, always discreetly,
and started to become familiar with the small provincial
French towns that he talks about with a slight smile
tinged with both gratitude and detachment. Somehow
or other he managed to get casual building jobs. Out
of €200 earned by helping to do up an old house, he
sent €20 to his mother in Khartoum and, above all, he
made sure he did not tell her about all this – too much
sadness, too much anxiety.

May your prayers enfold my fear
But
I do not deserve the name of body
Since this is my rotting corpse you see before you
This body rejected so many times it has become a
     carcass
The clearest water no longer reaches me
Even your dogs look at me strangely
Those dogs wrapped up warm and with their identity
     papers
And their names
Their cushions and collars adorned with pearls
Watching me strangely
O god whom I respect
When will you grant me your mercy
And allow my heart to stop
My heart full of poisoned flowers
This sphere which never tires
Whose beating wearies and enrages me
No harsher word than refugee can be thrown in a
     man's face

His papers are not 'in order' and, at the time of writing, he is under an order to leave French territory (OQTF, Obligation de quitter le territoire français), but he remains determined and has no intention of giving up. He has fixed his sights on a glimmer of hope, which tells him that he will eventually escape from 'this body rejected so many times it has become a carcass'. He has managed to get help and shelter from people in Paris and in smaller towns, albeit without forming close links with them. What sort of stranger is he? He is always an outsider, always in the process of arriving somewhere, officially an intruder (inside and outside), always trying to obtain the papers and the formalities that will allow him to settle in peace somewhere, to truly cross the border. His position on the 'foreigner' axis is very low, given that he is constantly having to slip under the radar of the French law on asylum and immigration, but he has managed to form a small social circle among those fortunate enough to have full citizenship, and these, along with some Sudanese friends and other poets of contemporary exile, bring him their support. Finally, in the midst of all this uncertainty about place and status, he manages to observe things 'through the eyes of a poet', like a stranger already battle-hardened, who is discovering the languages of others and their 'normal way' of living and thinking. He does this in the worst possible conditions for writing but, because his poems are heard, read, translated, and heard once more, his words reach out to a broader community, which, like himself, is a hybrid one. By watching us observing him as an *alien*, he holds up a mirror and frees Hassan's weary body from his personal hell and his longing for death. In real life he is full of hope and ingenuity, and the fact that he looks through the eyes of a stranger gives him a deeper understanding of the world and fixes a slight smile permanently on his face, as though he were watching from the sidelines.

Between the stranger who is becoming more and more cosmopolitan and the stranger who is slipping further and further into the dark depths of the alien, nothing is ever finished or fixed, and the cursors indicating exteriority, extraneity, and strangeness are in constant movement. The rejection, confinement, and death of aliens is a cry for help in response to which other people offer their hospitability, even if their societies have lost the meaning and the social practice of hospitality, and even if the combined imaginations and joint efforts of local people cannot hope to compensate for the hostility of their nation-states. What should be done to banish forever this spectre of the absolute and radicalised stranger, the alien, and to open the door instead to the stranger who has equal rights simply by virtue of belonging to the same world as anyone else? It is merely a matter of pushing all three cursors to the top end of the axis: increased freedom of movement, increased rights of belonging (perhaps extending this belonging to the entire planet), increased knowledge and recognition of the other and of shared cultures.

Conclusion

As it develops and strengthens, contemporary hospitality will undoubtedly take on new forms and new meanings, distinct from those represented by the anthropological and philosophical tradition but still connected to it. Today it takes the form of a social mobilisation, which is reinvigorating and revitalising societies now more individualized than in the past, and with less extensive families and less space, time and resources to 'sacrifice' to their guests, whether these are people they are close to or more distant. This new wave of enthusiasm has highlighted the need for relational contexts that can provide a certain level of security and help to integrate and bring meaning to the practice of hospitality at an individual level, where this practice is generally experienced as spontaneous, ethical or unconditional. While many practices reproduce situations involving 'overlapping' and openings between different social worlds (internal and external, private and public) that are typical of hospitality in general, others are innovative. In this way the development of local associations provides the missing link that fills the gap left between 'us' and the others by the compartmentalisation of private spheres, or reveals the existence of supportive social fabrics previously 'left dormant', as we saw in the context of village-based hospitality.

In these local practices – whether domestic or in the context of local associations, municipal, and so on – hospitality represents an accumulation of gestures that eventually unsettles politics, which, for its part, operates on a terrain and in a realm of imagination that is always national. But what exactly is this politics of – or within – hospitality? It is first of all one that is generated by the three-part relationship I have referred to above, where the decision to welcome a migrant is triggered by my opposition to the hostility shown by my state, or by its refusal to take action. The gesture becomes increasingly politicised, especially as the state opposes or condemns it. In this politicising process, dissatisfaction with the government implies that something more is expected of it. Hospitality takes on a different political meaning when it entails the choice of another way of life, one that is less urbane, less individualised, less dependent on established structures. It is the sign of an immediate form of politics, one determined to institute for itself other rules of solidarity and to bring together a 'community' (network, village, district), which goes against the principles championed by distant and hostile governments with their focus solely on the defence of the nation, of identity, of territory ...

Hospitality is not therefore either by nature or ontologically apolitical. The politics involved in it or underlying it depends on the contexts and conflicts within which it is offered. In Europe, it is no longer possible to mention hospitality, the provision of welcome or refuge cities, for example, without immediately conjuring up the closing of borders, migrants being turned away, camps unfit for purpose, xenophobic campaigns, or a refusal to allow certain categories or nationalities of foreigners to enter – in other words, without conjuring up the political polemics in which these forms of welcome immediately find their place.

Nevertheless, today as yesterday, hospitality is still a favour. For those who are made welcome, it is a relationship built on exchange, an asymmetrical one, where the two parties cannot both be equal at the same time and where passing strangers run the risk at any moment of being reduced simply to their absence of rights, either as a result of failings on the part of the host or because of hostility from a state that, for one reason or another, is determined to see them driven out of the national territory.

So who exactly is targeted by this injunction to respect 'the duty of hospitality' that operates in opposition to the policy of hostility shown by the nation-states? If it is addressed to local people, this issue, as we have already seen, has become the focus of a genuine social mobilisation. If it is addressed to states, I believe it will be the target of all sorts of linguistic and political manipulation – as demonstrated, for example, by the Turkish leader Tayyip Erdogan, who describes Syrian refugees as his 'guests', his younger brothers even, in the context of a dreamt-of return to the days of the Ottoman Empire and of state control over the associative sector, while at the same time negotiating contributions towards his national hospitality from European countries to the tune of millions of euros.[1]

From the perspective of the migrants scattered along the treacherous roads that take them from one country to another, the duty of hospitality cannot, in the long term, guarantee them any durable safe conduct. Only a *right* to hospitality in a cosmopolitical context would be able to compensate for the deadlock in discretionary migration policies and for the criminally reprehensible tactics of diplomatic bargaining. A move from the duty of some to the right of others would entail transposing the ideal of universal hospitality, a cause that is mobilising a growing number of citizens, into a rule of law stating that any stranger has the right not to be treated as an enemy, to use Kant's words, and imposed as an 'enforceable law' at a national level – which, on this subject as on others (notably, environmental issues),[2] is always the last to act.

'Our concern here is not with philanthropy but with *right*', warned Kant.[3] Our concern, even more acutely today than yesterday, is with political realism: the institution of hospitality is neither moral nor natural, writes Étienne Tassin, it is a 'pure understanding of the world, which prevents war and creates the conditions of peace'.[4] In a cosmopolitical context, law is placed above morality, in order to establish a principle that is at the same time universal and pragmatic. There is a growing wealth of proposals and debates on this issue. 'The right to mobility: a fundamental human right' (Catherine Wihtol de Wenden), 'hospitality as a regulatory juridical principle of human mobility' (Mireille Delmas-Marty), 'freedom of movement' (Migreurop), and other expressions show that the 'universality of law' is emerging from the current conflicts as a possible horizon.[5] By transforming the way strangers are perceived, but also the political attitude adopted towards them, we are opening up a new avenue that enables a switch from favour to right and allows us to begin thinking of the world as a common project.

*

The case of women and men caught up in migration who, wherever they are in the world, find themselves living in uncertain material or legal conditions and have not really chosen their mobility but have instead been forced to leave their homes for political, economic, or environmental reasons still represents only a minority among the 250 million people who reside in a country other than the one in which they were born. Yet these numbers are rising and will continue to do so according to all predictions, both as a consequence of globalisation (which opens up unhoped-for perspectives but destroys fragile local systems) and as a result of the repeated failures of the nation-states to take charge of the present and the future of the world in its totality and what will, from now on, be its *constant mobility*. This is why the case of migrants, even though a minority one, has a significance that reaches far beyond what it represents in its own right. It is clear that a new form of nomadism is in the process of emerging, one that forces us to reconsider the gaze, whether ancestral, philosophical, or anthropological, that we turn on the stranger.

All societies and cultures have found themselves historically divided between the opposing forces that seek to open up for or shut out the other. This was the finding reached by Claude Lévi-Strauss in response to the request made to him by UNESCO at the beginning of the 1950s for a contribution to the fight against racial prejudice launched after the drama of the Second World War and the Shoah: ostracism or indifference towards other cultures, even to the extent of negating them altogether, seemed to him as inevitable as their cooperation, their opening up, and their transformation within the onward march of humanity. And Lévi-Strauss concluded: 'The exclusive fatality, the unique fault which can afflict a human group and prevent it from completely fulfilling its nature is to be alone.'[6]

We could content ourselves today with repeating this truth, and thus relativising the present time itself, with its dramas and its anger, within this anthropological timelessness. However, since the question is not in the past but still lies ahead of us, a distant gaze is not appropriate. On the one hand, need it be reiterated, more than 40,000 deaths have occurred at borders throughout the world since 2000, and they were accompanied by an (apparent) acceptance of the 'let die' approach that passes for political realism in the eyes of governments caught in the grip of a form of siege mentality. On the other hand, the experience widely shared by migrants is likely to last, and the condition of the stranger will become even more widespread. Our world is and will be more and more mobile and will 'produce' more and more strangers. The *outsider* is the first person we see and the one who raises the question of what will become of the 'intruder', of his or her difference and rights, in an ideological context that today remains largely sedentary and national and where this outsider is seen through a lens 'prefabricated' by the spectre of the alien. Yet the context is also that of the planet, one in which we are all called on to become strangers more often and where, more or less well received depending on the place and the circumstances, we will need to invent a nomadic citizenship for all.

Postscript

The Stranger after Covid-19

What impact will the Covid-19 world health crisis that began in January 2020 have on the issues – cosmopolitanism, the condition of the stranger, hospitality – explored in this book, originally written in 2018? It is of course impossible not to reflect on the possible impact of this crisis, just as at present it is equally impossible to grasp the full extent of its consequences until the relevant inquiries have been carried out. Even if we cannot yet envisage the 'world after' Covid-19, it is obvious that the fact that we are indeed referring to a 'world before ...' is in itself evidence of the dramatic and sudden change that has taken place. Zygmunt Bauman, whose absence is all the more acutely felt today, might well have guided us towards some areas for research worth investigating in the light of an event that he seemed to have anticipated. He would no doubt have shared my view that we were *already* immersed in a world of uncertainty, a world that was expecting a catastrophe but without knowing what form it would take and without attempting to be in any way prepared for it. Or was that very lack of preparedness in itself part of the catastrophe? It certainly contributes to a greater sense of panic in the face of the event in question, given that no measures had been put in place to prepare any kind of response to it. This failure to provide individuals with solid foundations, whether cognitive, material, or institutional, from which to deal with unforeseen events and natural accidents is a characteristic of what Bauman called 'liquid' society. When there is no solid framework to support and help individuals in the face of existential anxieties, fear becomes another name for uncertainty.

Over the course of the past few years, collapse theories – or what has been called in France in recent years 'collapsology' – have featured in numerous essays and have become almost a separate discipline within philosophy and cultural studies. The notion of disaster has caught on, as though something made us secretly want it to happen, or – and this comes to very much the same thing – as though it were the inescapable fate of an unbridled and unlimited capitalism (so-called neoliberalism) to lead the world towards its destruction. This kind of fatalism is, in my view, more frightening than the catastrophe itself. For even though we were expecting it, and because we saw it as our inevitable fate, we failed to prepare ourselves for it.

I will now turn my attention to the more direct issue of the stranger, which is explored in this book. With the Covid-19 pandemic, the health border has taken precedent over any other borders, and it seems likely that it will continue to exercise a biopolitical domination on social life across the entire planet through the practice of governing populations in the name of a control of biological life. This biopolitical future of the planet presupposes, of course, that no opposing force, either a vigilant and democratic scrutiny or a local or worldwide citizens movement, will react and curb this sombre and dystopian process. But it is important to assess the potential – and always avoidable – consequences of this state of exception if we are to justify the warning itself.

We need to be able to see the catastrophe clearly and to understand it in order to combat it.

All of this immediately raises a new issue, which has a dramatic impact on what I have chosen to focus on until now. The issue in question is this: Are we not all in the process of becoming strangers to each other, physically separated, locked inside our frightened bodies?

What was certainly true 'before' is that we are all in the process of becoming more and more *often* strangers, as a result of contacts, travel, encounters with people from different cultures and societies. Migrants, tourists, foreign workers, businessmen and -women, and students have all encountered this phenomenon on the basis of their own experience. As I have argued in this book, the concept of the stranger is not about identity but refers instead to a condition at a particular time and in a certain place, and within the context of a specific relationship. Each one of us is more – or less – of a stranger in relation to certain places and certain people than we are in relation to other places and people.

What has changed – or is in the process of changing if nothing is done to prevent it – with the Covid-19 pandemic and the emergency policies that have self-legitimised in this context, re-ordering the various strata of humanitarian and public health measures, is that the health border has now taken precedent over all others (linguistic, nation-state, social). The other has become a threat, and the term is reinforced by a certain health-based reality, even though modulated by uncertainty. If everyone represents a threat to everyone else, but afflicted individuals still cannot be isolated and treated without regard to all their other characteristics (social, cultural, political, etc.), then the 'old' reflexes (not so old in fact, but simply carried over from the 'world before') make a return. As a result, certain bodies will be (are already) perceived more as 'strangers' than others, and what emerges most clearly in this spontaneous, unconsidered, and skin-deep process of discrimination is that there is a symbolic link between the biological body and the social body. This is apparent in violent forms of discrimination, which are based on physical, phenotypic characteristics of appearance in general. The biologisation of social life – or the impact that biopolitics has on daily life – opens the way to racial violence. In a sense, this is an accelerated form of racialisation, as happened when the threat of coronavirus was transformed into the 'Chinese virus' and people assumed to be Asian were attacked and ostracised, or when homeless people and migrants on the streets of Paris were spontaneously avoided and kept at a distance because they were perceived as being contagious purely and simply on the grounds of how they were dressed, the colour of their skin, or their general appearance.

It is interesting to go back to the beginning of March 2020, when Europeans saw a surge in the public health measures introduced to deal with the spread of Covid-19. Everything culminated in a tendency to look inwards and to withdraw within the confines of national borders. At the same time, Turkey was threatening to allow 'millions of refugees' into Greece because Europe was refusing to provide aid in the context of its conflict with Syria. In total, fewer than 10,000 migrants actually turned up at the Greek border during this whole new episode of the hospitality crisis, but the 'moral panic' gave rise to increasingly violent reactions. European leaders no longer exercised any restraint in their official statements concerning migrants and showed scant consideration for human rights (in particular the right to asylum), for which Europe nevertheless claimed to be the staunchest champion. Official statements such as 'the border is closed, go away', 'migrants are putting themselves in danger' by taking even one more step, Greece is the 'shield' of

Europe were all heard. Humanitarian language had been completely eclipsed by what seemed to be the 'self-evident' need for the measures taken by European countries, ostensibly in the interest of public health but at the same time unmistakably xenophobic, demonstrating at the same time the political hypocrisy around the use of such language ever since the end of the 1990s. A meticulous investigation by the Forensic Architecture team was able to prove that real bullets were fired on migrants at the Greek border, leaving seven injured and one dead.[1]

In times of catastrophe, it is not simply a matter of renewing our thinking. Even when the impact is violent enough to stir sluggish consciences and it is clear that a rethink is necessary, the latter remains couched in the words, concepts, and political reasoning that were available in 'the world before'. And it is then that the inherent danger of these words, concepts, and political reasoning is most clearly evident.

Notes

Notes to Introduction
1 J.-L. Nancy, 'The Intruder', in J.-L. Nancy, *Corpus.* New York: Fordham University Press, 2008, pp. 161–2.
2 W. Brown, *Walled States, Waning Sovereignty.* New York: Zone Books, 2010.
3 R. Schérer, *Zeus hospitalier: Éloge de l'hospitalité.* Paris: La Table Ronde, 2005, p. 19.

Notes to Chapter 1
1 According to Article L622-1 of the French law governing the entry and residence of foreigners in France and according to the Right to Asylum (CESEDA), any person who has, 'through direct or indirect assistance, facilitated or attempted to facilitate the illegal entry, movement, or residence of a foreigner in France' risks a five-year prison sentence and a fine of €30,000. On 6 July 2018 the constitutional council declared this decree to be anti-constitutional on the grounds of contradicting the (constitutional) principle of fraternity, and therefore to require amendment.
2 J. Derrida, *Cosmopolitans of the World, Unite!* Strasbourg, 1996. https://rm.coe.int/09000016808bf0c2 (translated in the context of the First Congress of the Cities of Asylum organized by the Council of Europe); J. Derrida and A. Dufourmantelle, *Of Hospitality: Anne*

Dufourmantelle Invites Jacques Derrida to Respond. Stanford, CA: Stanford University Press, 2000; M. Seffahi (ed.), *Autour de Jacques Derrida: De l'hospitalité.* Genouilleux: La Passe du vent, 2001.

3 F. Dupont, *L'Antiquité, territoire des écarts: Entretiens avec Pauline Colonna D'Istria et Sylvie Taussig.* Paris: Albin Michel, 2013, pp. 143–50.

4 J. Derrida 'Accueil, éthique, droit et politique' (conversation with Michel Wieviorka), in Seffahi, *Autour de Jacques Derrida,* pp. 186–7.

5 Dupont, *L'Antiquité, territoire des écarts,* p. 146.

6 Ibid., p. 148.

7 Ibid., p. 145. The difference is embodied socially in the two-sided Latin notion of *hospes–hostis* ('host'–'enemy').

8 É. Beneniste, *Indo-European Language and Society.* Book 1: *Economy.* London: Faber and Faber, 1973, p. 77.

9 Ibid., p. 79.

10 Derrida and Dufourmantelle, *Of Hospitality,* pp. 29 and 41.

11 Seffahi, *Autour de Jacques Derrida,* pp. 187–8.

12 Schérer, *Zeus hospitalier: Éloge de l'hospitalité.* Paris: La Table Ronde, 2005, p. 34, quoting from Homer, *Odyssey* 14, lines 61–4 (here in Robert Fitzgerald's translation of the *Odyssey,* London: Vintage, 2007, p. 249).

13 Plato, *Laws,* translated by Trevor Saunders. London: Penguin, 1975, p. 148 (= book 5, 730a); see also Schérer, *Zeus hospitalier,* p. 34.

14 G. Le Blanc, 'Politiques de l'hospitalité'. *Cités* 46 (2011): 87–97.

15 Ibid., p. 92. An infrapolitics which the author distinguishes from the 'super-politics of cosmopolitan aspirations'.

16 Plato, *Laws,* p. 148 (= 729e); see Schérer, *Zeus hospitalier,* p. 16.

17 Benveniste, *Indo-European Language and Society,* p. 77.

18 J. Derrida, 'Une hospitalité sans condition' (conversation with Michel Wieviorka), in Seffahi, *Autour de Jacques Derrida,* p. 176.

19   Derrida, 'Accueil, éthique, droit et politique', p. 188.

20   Ibid.

21   M. Bessone, 'Le Vocabulaire de l'hospitalité est-il républicain?'. *Éthique Publique* 17.1 (2015).

22   B. Boudou, 'Au nom de l'hospitalité: Les enjeux d'une rhétorique morale ou politique'. *Cités* 68 (2016): 33–48, here p. 34.

23   Schérer, *Zeus hospitalier*, p. 45.

24   P. Bourdieu, 'The social uses of kinship', in P. Bourdieu, *The Logic of Practice*. Stanford, CA: Stanford University Press, 1990, pp. 162–99, here p. 169.

25   J. Pitt-Rivers, *The Fate of Shechem, or the Politics of Sex: Essays in the Anthropology of the Mediterranean*. Cambridge: Cambridge University Press, 1977, p. 109.

26   Ibid., p. 107.

27   Ibid., pp. 104–5.

28   [Translator's note: in French, the word *hôte*, which means both guest and host, can be linked to the word *hostilité* ('hostility', 'enmity'). This reflects the relation, in Latin, between its etymon, *hostis*, and the derivative *hostilitas*.]

29   Pitt-Rivers, *Fate of Shechem*, p. 111.

30   A. Gotman, *Le Sens de l'hospitalité: Essais sur les fondements sociaux de l'accueil de l'autre*. Paris: PUF, 2001, and A. Gotman (ed.), *Villes et hospitalité: Les municipalités et leurs 'étrangers'*. Paris: Éditions de la MSH, 2004.

31   Dupont, *L'Antiquité, territoire des écarts*, p. 146.

32   Schérer, *Zeus hospitalier*, p. 158.

33   A. Gotman, 'La question de l'hospitalité aujourd'hui'. *Communications* 65 (1997): 5–19, here p. 11.

34   Schérer, *Zeus hospitalier*, p. 25.

35   M. Mauss, *The Gift: The Form and Reason for Exchange in Archaic Societies*. London: Routledge, 1990, p. 23.

36   The term 'quasi-kinship' was suggested by the British anthropologist M. G. Smith in his 'Exchange and marketing among the Hausa', in P. Bohannan and G. Dalton (eds), *Markets in Africa*, Evanston, IL: Northwestern University Press, 1962, pp. 299–334.

37   Gotman, *Le Sens de l'hospitalité*; see also A. Gotman,

'Les Périls de l'asymétrie: L'étranger est-il soluble dans l'immigré?'. *Pardes* 52 (2013): 15–36.

38 Pitt-Rivers, *Fate of Schechem*, p. 111.

39 Ibid.

40 A. Monsutti, 'Les Désillusions de l'hospitalité ou la mobilité comme acte politique', paper delivered to the seminar *Anthropologies de l'hospitalité* (conducted by Michel Agier, EHESS) on 16 January 2018.

41 J.-L. Nancy, *Corpus*, New York: Fordham University Press, 2008.

42 Schérer, *Zeus hospitalier*, p. 95, citing *The History of Byzantium* by Priscus, who accompanied Maximinus, the envoy of the Eastern Roman Emperor Theodosius, on a diplomatic mission to the court of Attila (mid-fifth century).

43 B. Saladin d'Anglure, 'Enfants nomades aux pays des Inuit Iglulik'. *Anthropologie et Sociétés* 12 (1988): 125–66.

44 See C. Fonseca, 'La Circulation des enfants pauvres au Brésil: Une pratique locale dans un monde globalisé'. *Anthropologie et Sociétés* 24.3 (2000): 53–73; M. Agier, 'Le Sexe de la pauvreté: Hommes, femmes et familles dans un "avenida" à Salvador de Bahia'. *Cahiers du Brésil Contemporain* 8 (1989): 81–112. (Republished in *Brésil(s)* O [2011]: 57–80.)

45 For more detail on the 'sociography of networks' in urban settings, see U. Hannerz, *Exploring the City: Inquiries towards an Urban Anthropology*. New York: Columbia University Press, 1980, and my own observations in M. Agier, *Anthropologie de la ville*. Paris: PUF, 2015, pp. 80–90.

46 S. Djigo, *Les Migrants de Calais: Enquête sur la vie en transit*. Marseilles: Agon, 2016, p. 149. See also Bessone, 'Le Vocabulaire de l'hospitalité est-il républicain?'.

47 S. Djigo, *Les Migrants de Calais*, p. 169.

48 W. Brown, *Walled States, Waning Sovereignty*. New York: Zone Books, 2010.

Notes to Chapter 2

1 I am referring to ongoing research that I shall comment on only briefly here. The complete results of this joint

inquiry on hospitality, conducted in the context of the Babels programme 'Towns as borders' (EHESS and the Agence nationale de la recherche, 2016–18) will be published in the series 'Bibliothèque des frontières' under the title *Hospitalité en France*, edited by M. Agier, M. Gerbier-Aublanc, and E. Masson-Diez. Neuvy: Le Passager clandestin, 2019.

2   See M. Gerbier-Aublanc, 'Un migrant chez soi', *Esprit* 446 (2018): 122–9.

3   See https://www.euractiv.fr/secion/politique/news/laccueil-de-migrants-par-les-citoyens-destabilise-le-gouvernement-belge.

4   Ibid.

5   See V. Bontemps, C. Makeremi, and S. Mazouz (eds), *Entre accueil et rejet: Ce que les villes font aux migrants.* Lyon: Le Passsager clandestin, 2018 (esp. pp. 63–78). This is another Babels project.

6   They have been described in more detail in M. Agier, *Les Migrants et nous: Comprendre Babel.* Paris: CNRS Éditions, 2016.

7   The two speakers in question were Éric Fassin and Odile Henry. I was present at this event and had been invited to speak, along with several other teachers and researchers and members of local associations and community groups.

8   See https://sursaut-citoyen.org and M. Baumard, 'Migrants: Le réseau d'hébergement citoyen s'étoffe'. *Le Monde*, 10 May 2017.

9   See the research carried out on this subject by D. Ristic, 'Trasiti i Favoriti ('Come in and Help Yourselves'): La Calabre, une terre d'hospitalité? Accueil des réfugiées et demandeurs d'asile au sein de villages socialement disqualifiés d'une région du Mezzogiorno'. MA thesis, EHESS, 2017 (this research is ongoing). See also the documentary made by S. Aiello and C. Catella, *Un paese di Calabria* (2016).

10 See M. Cosnay, *Jours de répit à Baïgorri.* Grâne: Gréaphis, 2017.

11 See various research and activity projects that have been supported by the Plan Urbanisme Construction Architecture (PUCA) over the last few years.

12 See M. Agier, *Campement urbain: Du refuge nait le ghetto*, Paris: Payot, 2013.

13 N. Puig and K. Doraï, 'Insertions urbaines et espaces relationnels des migrants et réfugiés au Proche-Orient', in N. Puig and K. Doraï, *L'Urbanité des marges: Migrants et réfugiés dans les villes du Proche-Orient.* Paris: Téraèdre, 2012, pp. 11–25, here p. 15.

14 L. Wirth, *The Ghetto.* Chicago, IL: University of Chicago Press, 1956. See R. Hutchinson and B. D. Haynes (eds), *The Ghetto: Contemporary Global Issues and Controversies.* New York: Routledge, 2018.

15 See M. Agier, Y. Bouagga, M. Galisson, C. Hanappe, M. Pette, and P. Wannesson, *The Jungle: Calais's Camps and Migrants.* Cambridge: Polity, 2019.

16 For further details on this case and on population movements in the region, see M. Agier, 'Parcours dans un paysage flottant de frontières'. *Revue Européenne des Migrations Internationales* 30 (2014): 13–23, and A. Dahdah and N. Puig (eds), *Exils syriens: Parcours et ancrages (Liban, Turquie, Europe).* Lyon: Le Passager clandestin, 2018.

17 The sociologist Isabelle Coutant describes this situation both from the point of view of someone living in the area and as an ethnographer of the event and of the affect it had on local life; see I. Coutand, *Les Migrants en bas de chez soi* (Paris: Seuil, 2018). The following two paragraphs are based on her book.

18 Ibid., p. 11.

19 Ibid., p. 204.

20 [Translator's note: Emmaüs is an international movement founded in 1949 by Abbé Pierre to support the homeless and to fight poverty.]

21 J. Derrida, *Cosmopolitans of the World, Unite!* Strasbourg 1996. https://rm.coe.int/09000016808bf0c2 (translated as part of the First Congress of Cities of Asylum).

22 F. Furri, 'Villes-refuge, ville rebelles et néomuncipalisme'. *Plein Droit* 115 (issue 'Villes et hospitalités'), 2017, here p. 4.

23 Ibid.

Notes to Chapter 3

1 R. Schérer, *Zeus hospitalier*. Paris: La Table ronde, 2005, p. 81. See also G. Noiriel, *La Tyrannie du national*. Paris: Calmann-Lévy, 1991.

2 F. Wolf, *Trois Utopies contemporaines*. Paris: Fayard, 2016, p. 145.

3 See M. Augé, *L'Avenir des terriens: Fin de la préhistoire de l'humanité comme société planétaire*. Paris: Albin Michel, 2017 and B. Latour, *Down to Earth: Politics in the New Climatic Regime*. Cambridge: Polity, 2018.

4 L. Carlier, 'Les Apports de Robert Park pour une approche sociologique du cosmopolitanisme'. *EspacesTemps.net*. https://www.espacestemps.net/en/articles/les-apports-de-park-pour-une-approche-sociologique-du-cosmopolitisme. On the approach taken by G. Simmel, see also G. Truc, 'Simmel, sociologique du cosmopolitanism', *Tumultes* 24 (2005): 49–77.

5 I. Kant, *Perpetual Peace and Other Essays*. Indianapolis, IN: Hackett, 1988, pp. 36 and 38.

6 Z. Bauman has devoted a considerable amount of research and study to this tendency to polarize the world – between tourists and vagabonds, or between 'the global' and 'the local' – which can only logically find strength and justification by diminishing the human rights of part of the world population. See in particular Z. Bauman, *Wasted Lives. Modernity and its Outcasts*. Cambridge: Polity, 2004 as well as his contribution to *The Great Regression*, Cambridge: Polity, 2017.

7 [Translator's note: Kant, *Perpetual Peace*, p. 138 (= para 358).]

8 U. Beck, 'Nationalisme méthodologique: Cosmopolitisme méthodologique: Un changement de paradigme dans les sciences sociales'. *Raisons Politiques* 54 (2014): 103–20.

9 M. Belissa and F. Gauthier, 'Kant, le droit cosmopolitique et la société civile des nations'. *Annales Historiques de la Révolution Française* 317 (1999): 495–511.

10 É. Tassin, *Un monde commun: Pour une cosmo-politique des conflits*. Paris: Seuil, 2016.

11 Tassin, *Un monde commun*, p. 18.

12 É. Balibar, *Secularism and Cosmopolitanism: Critical*

Hypothesis on Religion and Politics. New York: Columbia University Press, 2018, p. 22.

13 É. Glissant, *Treatise on the Whole World*. Liverpool: Liverpool University Press, 2020. [Translator's note: Edouard Glissant was a Caribbean writer, poet, philosopher, and literary critic. In this book he sets out his concept of what he calls *tout-monde*, according to which the whole world is seen as a network of interacting communities where we are all in relation to one another.] Following the thread of this inspiration and updating it, see also P. Chamoiseau, *Migrant Brothers: A Poet's Declaration of Human Dignity*. New Haven, CT: Yale University Press, 2018.

14 M. Fœssel and L. Lourme, 'Peut-on tenir ensemble le cosmopolitisme et la démocratie?', in M. Fœssel and L. Lourme, *Cosmopolitisme et démocratie*. Paris: PUF, 2016, here p. 6.

15 Ibid., p. 7.

16 See H. Arendt, *The Origins of Totalitarianism*. Part 2: *Imperialism*. San Diego: Harcourt, 1973. On the production of different legal categories of exile, see M. Agier and A-V. Madeira (eds), *Définir les réfugiés*. Paris: PUF, 2017.

17 Fœssel and Lourme, 'Peut-on tenir ensemble le cosmopolitisme et la démocratie ?', p. 8.

18 Ibid.; see U. Beck, *Cosmopolitan Vision*. Cambridge: Polity, 2006.

19 And, of course, Covid-19. This book was originally written in 2018, before the pandemic. See the postscript.

20 Translation and translators consequently have a *central* role in the experience of border situations and in the search for indispensable linguistic and symbolic overlapping. This is demonstrated by Barbara Cassin in her *Éloge de la traduction: Compliquer l'universel*. Paris: Fayard, 2016. On the thickness of the border and the diversity of its definitions, see M. Agier, *Borderlands: Towards an Anthropology of Cosmopolitan Condition*. Cambridge: Polity, 2016.

21 N. Glick Schiller, L. Basch, and C. Szanton Blanc, 'From immigration to transmigrant: Theorizing transnational

migration'. *Anthropological Quarterly* 68 (1995): 48–63.

22 A. Tarrius, *Les nouveaux cosmopolites*. La Tour-d'Aigues: Éditions de l'Aube, 2000.

23 G. Lins Ribeiro, 'Economic globalization from below'. *Ethnográfica* 10.2 (2006): 233–49.

24 C. Schmoll, 'Cosmopolitisme au quotidien et circula-tions commerciales à Naples'. *Cahiers de la Mediterrané* 67 (2003): 345–60.

25 N. Glick Schiller and A. Irving, *Whose Cosmopolitanism? Critical Perspectives, Relationalities and Discontents*. New York: Berghahn Books, 2015.

26 Cassin, *Éloge de la traduction*.

27 See M. Agier, Y. Bouagga, M. Galisson, C. Hanappe, M. Pette, and P. Wannesson, *The Jungle: Calais's Camps and Migrants*. Cambridge: Polity, 2019, and the film *L'Héroïque lande: La frontière brûle*, directed by Nicolas Klotz and Élizabeth Perceval (2017).

Notes to Chapter 4

1 D. Letort, 'America, America (Elia Kazan, 1963): La mémoire de l'exil'. *Quaina* 3 (2012).

2 J.-L. Nancy, *Corpus*. New York: Fordham University Press, pp. 161–2.

3 S. Cerutti, *Étrangers: Étude d'une condition d'incertitude dans une société d'Ancien Régime*. Montrouge: Bayard, 2012.

4 Ibid., p. 23.

5 G. Simmel, 'The Stranger', in G. Simmel, *On Individuality and Social Forms*. Chicago, IL: University of Chicago Press, 1971, pp. 143–9, here p. 143.

6 Ibid., p.145.

7 J. Bazin, 'Interpréter ou décrire: Notes critiques sur la connaissance anthropologique', in J. Revel and N. Wachtel (eds), *Une école pour les sciences sociales: De la VIème section à l'École des hautes études en sciences sociales*. Paris: Cerf, 1996, pp. 401–20. (Also published in J. Bazin, *Des clous dans la Joconde: L'anthropologie autrement*. Toulouse: Anacharsis, 2008, pp. 407–33.)

8   See M. Agier, *Les Migrants et nous: Comprendre Babel*. Paris: CNRS Éditions, 2016.

9   A. Schütz, 'The Stranger: An Essay in Social Psychology'. *American Journal of Sociology* 49.6 (1944): 499–507.

10 B. Cassin, *Éloge de la traduction*. Paris: Fayard, 2016.

11 *Spectres Are Haunting Europe*, directed by M. Kourkouta and N. Giannari (2016). The voice-over, by N. Giannari, was published and discussed by Georges Didi-Huberman in his *Passer quoi qui'il en coûte*. Paris: Minuit, 2017.

12 *Ta'ang*, directed by Wang Bing (2016).

13 And also in the migrant camp in Calais in 2015–16. See *The Wild Frontier*, directed by N. Klotz and E. Perceval (2017).

14 I came across Hassan Yacine thanks to Chowra Makaremi, sociologist at the CNRS and member of the Babels programme. She had met him herself in the context of research on the movement associated with the encampments in north Paris. The poem 'La Malédiction', translated from Arabic into French by Helmi Trad, some extracts of which are cited here, was published in full in V. Bontemps, C. Makeremi, and S. Mazouz (eds), *Entre accueil et rejet: Ce que les villes font aux migrants*. Lyon: Le Passsager clandestin, 2018, pp. 59–62. It was also included, along with two other poems by the same author, in *Tumultes* 51.2 (2018). The English version cited here is translated from the French by Helen Morrison for this volume.

Notes to Conclusion

1   See See V. Bontemps, C. Makeremi, and S. Mazouz (eds), *Entre accueil et rejet: Ce que les villes font aux migrants*. Lyon: Le Passsager clandestin, 2018, pp. 101–16.

2   See M. Delmas-Marty, *Résister, responsabiliser, anticiper*. Paris: Seuil, 2013.

3   E. Kant, *Perpetual Peace and Other Essays*. Indianopolis, IN: Hackett Publishing, 1988, p. 117.

4   É. Tassin, 'Philosophie/et/politique de la migration'. *Raison Publique* 21 (2017): 197–215, here p. 209.

5   D. Lochak, *Face aux migrants: État de droit ou état*

de siège? Paris: Textuel, 2007, p. 59 (interview with Bertand Richard).

6 C. Lévi-Strauss, 'Race and History', in C. Lévi-Strauss, *Structural Anthropology*, vol. 2. Harmondsworth: Penguin, 1978, p. 356.

Note to Postscript

1 Visit https://forensic-architecture.org/investigation/the-killing-of-muhammad-gulzar.

Index